40 COMPREHENSION EXERCISES IN ENGLISH

R. E. HOUSEMAN
M.A., LONDON, M.ED., MANCHESTER

HULTON EDUCATIONAL
PUBLICATIONS

© R. E. HOUSEMAN
1958
Reprinted 1959
Reprinted 1960
Reprinted 1963
Reprinted 1966
Reprinted 1969
Reprinted 1970
Reprinted 1972
Reprinted 1974
Reprinted 1977
Reprinted 1978

ISBN 0 7175 0188 4 (Pupils)
      0 7175 0189 2 (Teachers)

*Published by Hulton Educational Publications Ltd.,
Raans Road, Amersham, Bucks.*
Printed in Malta by Interprint (Malta) Ltd.

ACKNOWLEDGEMENTS

For permission to print extracts, grateful thanks are due to the following authors, publishers and owners of copyright:—

Messrs. A. P. Watt & Son and Mr. J. M. Orczy-Barstow for *The Scarlet Pimpernel* by Baroness Orczy; with the Tweedsmuir Trustees for *Greenmantle* by John Buchan; with the executors of the late Mr. H. G. Wells for *The Invisible Man* and *The First Men in the Moon* by H. G. Wells; with the Rider Haggard executors for *King Solomon's Mines;* with Trinity College, Oxford, for *The Four Feathers* by A. E. W. Mason, and with J. M. Dent for *The Prisoner of Zenda* by Anthony Hope.

B. T. Batsford Ltd., for *A History of Flying* by C. H. Gibbs-Smith.

Messrs. Sampson Low, Marston & Co. Ltd., for *The Modern World Book of Railways* by Paul Townend.

Messrs. Collins (London), for *Sir Francis Drake* by James A. Williamson and Messrs. Collins (Glasgow) for *Britain's Wonderland of Nature—The Farmer as Nature Lover* by Doreen Wallace.

Messrs. Faber & Faber, for *Farmer's Glory* by A. G. Street.

Messrs. E. J. Arnold, Leeds, for *In Your Garden* by C. H. Middleton; *Pioneers of the Modern World* by E. H. Carter, on *Pasteur* and *Abraham Lincoln.*

Messrs. Allen & Unwin, for *The Children's Life of the Bee* by Maurice Maeterlinck.

Oxford University Press, for *The World. A General Regional Geography* by Jasper H. Stembridge, on *Canada* and on *Volcanoes;* and *Lark Rise to Candleford* by Flora Thompson.

A. Wheaton & Co. Ltd., Exeter, for *Modern Science Studies* by W. D. Barras.

Messrs. Collins and Messrs. Christy & Moore, for *South with Scott* by E. R. G. R. Evans.

Messrs. Hodder & Stoughton, for *The Ascent of Everest* by Sir John Hunt, *The Scarlet Pimpernel* by Baroness Orczy, and *Greenmantle* by John Buchan.

Messrs. Cassell & Co., for *Jump for Joy* by Pat Smythe and *King Solomon's Mines* by H. Rider Haggard.

Messrs. Crosby Lockwood & Son Ltd., for *Solid Fuel Housecraft* by Elspet Fraser-Stephen.

Messrs. D. C. Heath & Co., Boston, for *A Pan-American Journey* by E. L. Castrillo.

Raleigh Industries Ltd., Nottingham, for specification of "Raleigh Automatic Filter Switch Unit".

Messrs. Odhams Press, for *Wonders of Nature—Ants*; also *My Early Life* by Winston S. Churchill.

Messrs. George Harrap, for *Pioneers of Invention* by William and Stella Nida.

Evans Bros. Ltd., for *The Complete Book of Woodwork* by Charles H. Hayward.

Messrs. J. M. Dent & Sons Ltd., for *Three Men in a Boat* by Jerome K. Jerome.

Basil Blackwell, Oxford, for *Cue for Treason* by Geoffrey Trease.

Messrs. Edward Arnold (Publishers) Ltd., for *Moonfleet* by J. Meade Falkner.

Messrs. Jonathan Cape and the Federation Francaise de la Montagne, for *Annapurna* by Maurice Herzog.

Messrs. Chatto & Windus, for *Memoirs of a Mountaineer* by F. Spencer Chapman.

Messrs. Macmillan & Co. Ltd., with the Trustees of the Hardy Estate, for *Far from the Madding Crowd* by Thomas Hardy.

Messrs. Blackie & Son Ltd., for *Beyond the Burma Road* by Percy F. Westerman.

Messrs. J. M. Dent, for *Coco the Clown* by Himself.

Messrs. Methuen & Co. Ltd., for *In Search of England* by H. V. Morton.

University of London Press, for *Out with Romany* by G. Bramwell Evens.

B.B.C. Publications, 35 Marylebone High Street, London, W.1, for an extract from *The Radio Times*, April 11, 1958.

Royal Life-Saving Society's *Handbook of Instruction*, Desborough House, 14 Devonshire Street, Portland Place, W.1, for extract on *Shock*.

Messrs. Herbert Jenkins for *Right-Ho Jeeves* by P. G. Wodehouse.

CONTENTS

Exercise	Page
I.	7
II.	9
III.	11
IV.	14
V.	16
VI.	19
VII.	21
VIII.	24
IX.	27
X.	31
XI.	34
XII.	37
XIII.	40
XIV.	43
XV.	46
XVI.	49
XVII.	53
XVIII.	56
XIX.	59
XX.	62
XXI.	65
XXII.	68
XXIII.	71
XXIV.	75
XXV.	78
XXVI.	81
XXVII.	84
XXVIII.	87
XXIX.	91
XXX.	94
XXXI.	97
XXXII.	102
XXXIII.	105
XXXIV.	109
XXXV.	113
XXXVI.	117
XXVII.	121
XXXVIII.	125
XXXIX.	129
XL.	133

PREFACE

As in the author's "40 One-Word Tests in English", and "40 Lessons and Exercises in Grammar and Language", the answers to the questions are almost entirely objective. There are, however, variations and alternative answers which can be accepted according to the teacher's judgement. The majority of the answers, with few exceptions, can be obtained from the extracts themselves, but some questions are asked on closely-related topics.

In most cases, the source of the extract is given, so that where it appeals, it may encourage the pupil to further reading.

The Teacher's Combined Exercise and Answer Book makes speedy and accurate marking possible.

R. E. H.

1

(A) **Read carefully this extract from** *Treasure Island* **and then answer the questions that follow.**

> The night passed, and the next day, after dinner, Redruth and I were afoot again, and on the road. I said good-bye to mother and the cove where I had lived since I was born, and the dear old Admiral Benbow—since he was repainted, no longer quite so dear. One of my last thoughts was of the captain, who had so often strode along the beach with his cocked hat, his sabre-cut cheek, and his old brass telescope. Next moment we had turned the corner, and my home was out of sight.

1. Was the Admiral Benbow—a person, ship, or an inn?
2. What is a cove—a bay, peninsula, or shop?
3. How was the captain's face marked?
4. How did the writer travel—by rail, sea, or road?
5. To whom did the writer say "Good-bye"—to Redruth, the captain, his mother?
6. Who wrote *Treasure Island*—George Stephenson, John Buchan, Robert Louis Stevenson?
7. What do we call the person who writes a book—printer, publisher, author?
8. Write in full the name of the firm who *publishes* this book that you are now using.
9. How many pages has this book?

(B) **Now read this extract from** *The Water Babies* **and then answer the questions.**

> Now, Tom was a cunning little fellow—as cunning as an old Exmoor stag. Why not? Though he was but ten years old, he had lived longer than most stags, and had more wits to start with into the bargain.
>
> He knew as well as a stag that if he backed he might throw the hounds out. So the first thing he did when he was over the

wall was to make the neatest double sharp to his right, and run along under the wall for nearly half a mile.

Whereby Sir John, and the keeper, and the steward, and the gardener, and the ploughman, and the dairymaid, and all the hue-and-cry together, went on ahead half a mile in the very opposite direction, and inside the wall, leaving him a mile off on the outside; while Tom heard their shouts die away in the woods and chuckled to himself merrily.

1 What sort of boy was Tom—stupid, afraid, crafty?
2 Where is Exmoor—in Yorkshire, Derbyshire, Sussex, Devonshire?
3 Two animals are referred to in this extract. What are they?
4 How far did Tom run along the wall—a mile, nearly 800 yards, two miles?
5 In which direction did Tom's pursuers go—the same, opposite, or to the right?
6 What servants are mentioned in the extract?
7 What is meant by a 'hue and cry'?
8 When Tom had outwitted his pursuers what did he do?

(C) Read the following letter:—

"Greenmeadows",
Marshworth,
Lincoln.
Tuesday, March 4th, 1958.

Dear Alec,

Can you come to my birthday party next Friday? There will be thirteen candles on the cake.

George is coming, and my two cousins Olwyn and Trevor. Of course there will be my two sisters and little brother Terry and my Aunt Flo' and Mum.

Dad has to take two calves to market so he won't be able to join us till after tea.

I went to see a good film last Thursday. Dad drove us into Lincoln by car; the journey took about half-an-hour.

I wanted Frank to come to my party but he is ill.

Oh dear! I see I have missed the last post so my letter will have to wait until tomorrow.
Let me know if you are coming.
                    Yours sincerely,
                        Hugh.

Now answer the following questions:—

1 How old is Hugh this birthday?
2 Assuming that Alec accepts the invitation, how many sit down to tea?
3 Who was unable to come to the party?
4 What did Hugh's father do for a living—a butcher, chauffeur, farmer?
5 What date did Hugh go to the cinema?
6 Give the exact date of Hugh's birth.
7 Where was "Greenmeadows"—in the town, in the country, I cannot tell?
8 What part of the day did Hugh write his letter—morning, evening, I cannot tell?
9 What relation was Olwyn to Hugh's mother—cousin, grand-daughter, niece?
10 What day was Hugh's letter posted?

2

(A) **Read this extract from** *Black Beauty* **by Anna Sewell.**

My master was not immediately suited, but in a few days my new groom came. He was a tall, good-looking fellow enough; but if ever there was a humbug in the shape of a groom, Alfred Smirk was the man. He was very civil to me, and never used me ill: in fact, he did a great deal of stroking and patting when his master was there to see it. He always brushed my mane and tail with water, and my hoofs with oil before he brought me to the door, to make me look smart; but as to cleaning my feet, or looking to my shoes, or grooming me thoroughly, he thought no more of that than if I had been a cow. He left my bit rusty, my saddle damp, and my crupper stiff.

Now answer the following:—

1 Who is speaking—a servant, a horse, I do not know?

2 What is a groom—a man who gets married, a kind of brush, one who attends to the well-being of a horse?

3 What does the phrase mean, "never used me ill"—rode me when I was ill, made me ill, never did me any harm?

4 Why did the groom put oil on the horse's hoofs—to make them slippery, to keep them in good condition, to make them shine?

5 Where do you find a horse's mane—on its back, its tail, or on its neck?

6 Which part of the harness was rusty?

7 Which part of the harness was damp?

8 Which part of the harness was stiff?

9 In this passage what is the meaning of the word "humbug"—a kind of sweet, a bug that hums, a fraud?

10 What would you call this story—a legend, an autobiography, a biography?

(B) Here is a letter in which a boy says exactly the opposite of what he meant to say. Substitute the right word for each word underlined.

42, High Street,
China Town,
6th March, 1958.

My (1) hateful Tom,

I was very (2) ungrateful for the (3) horrible tea you gave me yesterday. I was very (4) happy all day until I received your (5) unwelcome letter. What a lot of (6) miserable friends you have, their conversation was most (7) ridiculous. Remember me to your (8) unkind mother, and (9) irritable sister.

(10) Never yours,
Dick.

(C)   Here is a plan of a family sitting at the dining table.

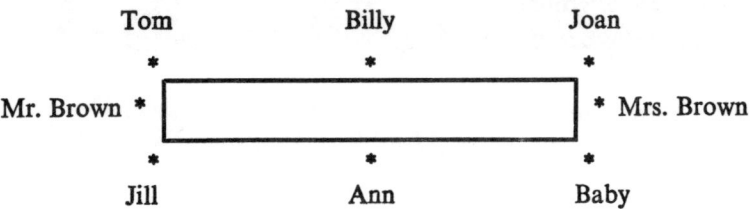

Answer the following questions:—
1 Who is sitting opposite Mrs. Brown?
2 Who is sitting on Ann's right?
3 Who is sitting between Tom and Joan?
4 Who is directly opposite Tom?
5 Who is on Mr. Brown's left?
6 Who is diagonally opposite to Joan?

3

(A) Read carefully these three verses from a poem called *The Windmill* by H. W. Longfellow and then answer the questions that follow.

BEHOLD! a giant am I!
Aloft here in my tower,
With my granite jaws I devour
The maize, and the wheat, and the rye,
And grind them into flour.

I look down over the farms;
In the fields of grain I see
The harvest that is to be,
And I fling to the air my arms,
For I know it is all for me.

I hear the sound of flails
Far off, from the threshing-floors
In barns, with their open doors,
And the wind, and the wind in my sails,
Louder and louder roars.

1 Where is the windmill probably situated—on a hill, in a valley, on a flat piece of ground?
2 What drives the windmill—steam, water, wind, electricity?
3 What is a flail used for—to thresh corn, to open doors, to crush wheat?
4 Did the barns have their doors—shut, open, ajar?
5 Name the three different kinds of grain mentioned.

(B) **Read carefully this extract from** *Uncle Tom's Cabin* **by Harriet Beecher Stowe. It is about a little girl called Topsy.**

> She was one of the blackest of her race; and her round shining eyes, glittering as glass beads, moved with quick and restless glances over everything in the room. Her mouth half open with astonishment at the wonders of the new mas'r's parlour, displayed a white and brilliant set of teeth. Her woolly hair was braided in sundry little tails which stuck out in every direction. The expression of the face was an odd mixture of shrewdness and cunning; over which was oddly drawn, like a kind of veil, an expression of the most doleful gravity and solemnity. She was dressed in a single, filthy, ragged garment, made of bagging; and stood with her hands demurely folded before her. Altogether there was something odd and goblin-like about her appearance—something, as Miss Ophelia afterwards said 'so heathenish', as to inspire that good lady with utter dismay.

Now answer the following questions:—

1 To what race of people do you think Topsy belonged?
2 Which words best describe her eyes?
3 Why was her mouth half-open?
4 What was the appearance of her teeth?
5 Give two adjectives describing her dress.
6 Her dress was of "bagging". What do you think this means?
7 Her general appearance was —— ?
8 Write the word "mas'r's" as we would say it.

(C) Read the following extract from that fascinating story of the French Revolution called *The Scarlet Pimpernel* by Baroness Orczy.

A beautiful starlit night had followed on the day of incessant rain; a cool summer's night, essentially English in its suggestion of moisture and scent of wet earth and dripping leaves.

The magnificent coach, drawn by four of the finest thoroughbreds in England, had driven off along the London Road, with Sir Percy Blakeney on the box, holding the reins in his slender feminine hands, and beside him Lady Blakeney wrapped in costly furs. A fifty-mile drive on a starlit summer's night! Marguerite had hailed the notion of it with delight . . . Sir Percy was an enthusiastic whip; his four thoroughbreds, which had been sent down to Dover a couple of days before, were just sufficiently fresh and restive to add zest to the expedition, and Marguerite revelled in anticipation of the few hours of solitude, with the soft night breeze fanning her cheeks. She knew from old experience that Sir Percy would speak little, if at all: he had often driven her on his beautiful coach for hours at night, from point to point, without making more than one or two casual remarks upon the weather or the state of the roads. He was very fond of driving by night, and she had very quickly adopted his fancy: as she sat next to him hour after hour, admiring the dexterous certain way in which he handled the reins, she often wondered what went on in that slow-going head of his. He never told her, and she had never cared to ask.

Now answer the following:—

1 What kind of night was it?
2 Describe a typical cool summer's night after rain.
3 Where was the coach being driven and for how far?
4 What is meant by 'thoroughbreds'?
5 What sort of driver was Sir Percy?
6 Was he very talkative when driving?
7 What is meant by 'casual remarks'?
8 What did Marguerite often wonder while Sir Percy was driving?

9   What part of speech is (a) magnificent, (b) wrapped, (c) anticipation, (d) never?

10 Give the word opposite in meaning to (a) feminine, (b) quickly, (c) never.

4

(A) **Read the following and then answer the questions.**

A Shopping Problem.

There were four sisters whose names were Judy, Jane, Jill and Joan. One day they went to town to choose some fabrics to make new dresses. The materials they selected were pale-pink silk, apple-green velvet, sprigged-muslin, and some brown woollen material.

Judy and Jill wanted flimsy dance frocks. Judy could not wear pink because it did not suit the colour of her hair. Jane wanted a warm frock but did not care for nigger-brown. Joan was a 'tom-boy' and wanted a frock which would stand hard wear and wouldn't show the dirt. Each girl chose a different material.

1 What material would Judy choose?
2 What material would Jane choose?
3 Who would choose pale-pink silk?
4 Which would be the best choice for Joan?

(B) Study the following:—

GINGERBREAD

Ingredients   12 ozs. self-raising flour.
1 teaspoonful ground ginger.
1 teaspoonful mixed spice.
6 ozs. sugar.
4 ozs. margarine.
2 tablespoonfuls dark treacle.
One egg, beaten with
One teacupful milk.

Method

First mix flour and spices. Beat the sugar and margarine to a cream, and stir in the treacle. Then add the dry ingredients and the beaten egg and milk alternately, a little at a time, and MIX THOROUGHLY. Pour into a shallow dripping tin and bake in a MODERATE OVEN about three-quarters of an hour. Cut into fingers or squares.

Variation

A little chopped lemon peel, preserved ginger, or a few raisins may be added if desired.

Now answer these questions:—

1. Is this an advertisement, recipe, or prescription?
2. Name TWO spices mentioned.
3. Name *three* dry ingredients.
4. Why are some directions written in BLOCK letters—because it looks imposing, because they are most important, because the cook may have poor eyesight?
5. Write out in full "ozs."
6. What is meant by a MODERATE OVEN—one that is neither too big nor too small, the temperature must be neither too high nor too low, an electric or gas oven?
7. Name any ONE thing that would make the gingerbread more interesting to eat.

(C) **Read the following extract "Gussie Presents the Prizes" by P. G. Wodehouse, an episode from the novel** *Right-Ho Jeeves.*

The hall was gaily decorated with flags and coloured paper, and the eye was further refreshed by the spectacle of a mixed drove of boys, parents, and what not, the former running a good deal to shiny faces and Eton collars, the latter stressing the black-satin note rather when female, and looking as if their coats were too tight, if male. And presently there was some applause—sporadic, Jeeves has since told me it was—and I saw Gussie being steered by a bearded bloke in a gown to a seat in the middle of the platform.

Now answer these questions:—

1. How was the hall decorated?
2. What especially did the boys wear?
3. How did their faces appear?
4. What effect did the clothes of the women produce?
5. How did the men appear to be dressed?
6. What do we call the people who attended the function?
7. What kind of applause was there at first?
8. Which is the slang word in the paragraph?

5

(A) Read carefully the following extract from *The Pied Piper of Hamelin*, by Robert Browning (1812-1889).

> Rats!
> They fought the dogs, and killed the cats,
> And bit the babies in the cradles,
> And ate the cheeses out of the vats,
> And licked the soup from the cook's own ladles,
> Split open the kegs of salted sprats,
> Made nests inside men's Sunday hats,
> And even spoiled the women's chats,
> By drowning their speaking
> With shrieking and squeaking
> In fifty different sharps and flats.
>
> At last the people in a body
> To the Town Hall came flocking:
> 'Tis clear', cried they, 'our Mayor's a noddy;
> And as for our Corporation—shocking
> To think we buy gowns lined with ermine
> For dolts that can't or won't determine
> What's best to rid us of our vermin!
> You hope, because you're old and obese,
> To find in the furry civic robe ease?

Rouse up, Sirs! Give your brains a racking
To find the remedy we're lacking,
Or, sure as fate, we'll send you packing.'
At this the Mayor and Corporation
Quaked with a mighty consternation.

Now answer these questions:—

1 What animals are mentioned in this extract?
2 What fish are mentioned?
3 What article of clothing is referred to?
4 State three things which we normally eat.
5 Which person named above usually works in the kitchen?
6 What two words might be used to describe a barrel or tub?
7 Where do we find objects known as "sharps and flats"?
8 To what place did the people flock?
9 How did they describe the Mayor?
10 What word did they use to describe members of the Corporation?
11 What did they threaten to do with them?
12 What line in the passage means 'trembled with fear'?

(B) Read the following and then answer the questions.
Brenda's Party.

Monday, 10th March, 1958.

Dear Brenda,
    I hope to be present at your party today week at 4 p.m. Jean came out of hospital only the day before yesterday, so I don't suppose she can come. I am having my party a fortnight tomorrow so I hope that you will come in return. It will be my fourteenth birthday then.

Yours,
Joyce.

1. When was Brenda's party?
2. When was Joyce's party?
3. When was Joyce born?
4. On what day did Jean come out of hospital?
5. How many days were there in the month just previous to March?
6. If the 10th March 1958 was on a Monday, what day was it on the 1st March 1958?

(C) **Read this little fable.**

THE FOX AND THE CROW.

A crow had snatched a goodly piece of cheese out of a window and flew with it into a high tree, intent on enjoying her prize. A fox spied the dainty morsel, and thus he planned his approaches. "O Crow," said he, "how beautiful are thy wings, how bright thine eye! how graceful thy neck! thy breast is the breast of an eagle! thy claws—I beg pardon—thy talons are a match for all the beasts of the field. O! that such a bird should be dumb, and want only a voice!"

The crow, pleased with the flattery, and chuckling to think how she would surprise the fox with her caw, opened her mouth—down dropped the cheese, which the fox snapping up, observed, as he walked away, that whatever he had remarked of her beauty, he had said nothing yet of her brains.

Men seldom flatter without some private end in view; and they who listen to such music may expect to have to pay the piper.

Now answer these questions:—

1. From where did the crow snatch the piece of cheese?
2. Where did the crow fly with the cheese?
3. The fox flattered the crow by referring to five different parts of its body. Name them.
4. Give any three adjectives the fox used to flatter the crow.
5. What made the crow open its mouth?
6. To what did the crow fall a victim?
7. What do you call the lesson learnt from a fable?

6

(A) Read the following extract from a first-aid book and then answer the questions:—

How to Treat Bruises

As soon as possible after receiving the injury, generally caused by a blow, knock, or fall, apply cold water, ice, or even cold metal, to the parts affected, as cold prevents the formation of a bruise by stopping the bleeding taking place under the skin.

Fresh butter is also an excellent remedy for bruises. Apply it immediately after the accident and continue for some time. Fresh butter will often prevent the ugly appearance of a "black eye" if applied at once.

Salad oil, too, can be recommended for bruises; tincture of arnica is another remedy; use one teaspoonful to a tumbler of water, and apply with a soft rag.

1 How are bruises usually caused?
2 How many remedies are mentioned here?
3 Name any small metal article which might be used to apply to a bruise.
4 If you have no fresh butter, what substitute mentioned here could you use?
5 Write down the names of the liquids which can be applied to bruises.
6 What is another name for 'tumbler'?
7 Write out the exact directions for using tincture of arnica.
8 State exactly when to apply any of the above remedies.

(B) Read this extract from *Coral Island* by R. M. Ballantyne and then answer the questions that follow.

It was a wild, black night of howling storm, the night on which I was born on the foaming bosom of the broad Atlantic Ocean. My father was a sea-captain; my grandfather was a sea-captain; my great-grandfather had been a marine. Nobody could tell positively what occupation his father had followed; but my dear mother used to assert that he had been a midshipman whose grandfather, on the mother's side, had been an admiral in the royal navy. At any rate, we knew that, as far back as our family could be traced, it had been intimately connected with the great watery waste. Indeed, this was the case on both sides of the house; for my mother always went to sea with my father on his long voyages, and so spent the greater part of her life upon the water.

Thus it was, I suppose, that I came to inherit a roving disposition. Soon after I was born, my father, being old, retired from a seafaring life, purchased a small cottage in a fishing village on the west coast of England, and settled down to spend the evening of his life on the shores of that sea, which had for so many years been his home. It was not long after this that I began to show the roving spirit that dwelt within me.

1 Where was the speaker born?
2 What was his father—a soldier, sailor, or marine?
3 Who had been an admiral?
4 What do we call those from whom we are descended?
5 Where was the speaker's mother usually to be found?
6 Give the word opposite in meaning to 'inherit'.
7 What did the writer inherit?
8 Where did the writer's father retire?
9 Why did he choose this place to retire?

(C) **Read carefully the following passage from** *A History of Flying* **by C. H. Gibbs-Smith and then answer the questions.**

But all other events were dwarfed when Louis Blériot, in his monoplane No. XI, took off from Barraques, on the French coast, on the morning of 25 July 1909, and landed safely near Dover Castle just over half an hour later. He thus won the *Daily Mail* £1,000 prize. That prize, however, had nearly gone to Hubert Latham, who attempted a crossing in his "Antoinette" monoplane on 19 July. But engine failure forced him down on to the sea, just short of the English coast, where he and his machine were rescued and taken back to France.

Blériot made headlines in the newspapers of the world and was fêted as a hero in London and Paris. It was this flight that struck such an ominous note in the Europe of that time. 'The day that Blériot flew the Channel', wrote Sir Alan Cobham, 'marked the end of our insular safety, and the beginning of the time when Britain must seek another form of defence besides its ships.'

More immediately the flight had the effect of popularizing the Blériot type of monoplane to such an extent that he was flooded with orders, and Blériot monoplanes were later bought by many Governments. The type XI was an aircraft of 25.5 feet span, a lifting surface of 150 square feet and an Anzani motor of 22-25 horse-power. She was underpowered with this engine, and pilots welcomed the installation of the 50 horse-power "Gnome" rotary engine, which from 1909-1914—and in various versions up to 100 horse-power—became one of the most famous of early aero-engines.

1 From what place on the French coast did Blériot take off?
2 Where did he land on the English coast?
3 About how long did the flight take him?
4 What did he win?
5 What did this flight mark an end of?
6 What was the immediate effect of Blériot's flight?
7 Name one of the most famous of early aero-engines.
8 Who nearly anticipated Blériot?

7

(A) **Read this extract "The Jackdaw of Rheims", from** *The Ingoldsby Legends* **by R. H. Barham, and then answer the questions below.**

The feast was over, the board was clear'd,
The flawns and the custards had all disappear'd
And six little Singing-boys,—dear little souls!

In nice clean faces, and nice white stoles,
Came in order due, two by two,
Marching that grand refectory through!
A nice little boy held a golden ewer,
Emboss'd and fill'd with water as pure
As any that flows between Rheims and Namur,
Which a nice little boy stood ready to catch
In a fine golden hand-basin made to match.
Two nice little boys, rather more grown,
Carried lavender-water, and eau de Cologne;
And a nice little boy had a nice cake of soap,
Worthy of washing the hands of the Pope.
One little boy more a napkin bore,
Of the best white diaper, fringed with pink,
And a Cardinal's hat mark'd in "permanent ink".

1 A word here means a kind of custard. What is it?
2 What word means a dining hall?
3 What two towns are mentioned and where are they situated?
4 What scents are referred to?
5 What did one little boy carry a napkin for?
6 What did the two bigger boys carry?
7 What was marked and with what liquid?
8 What is a ewer?

(B) **Read this extract from *A Christmas Carol* by Charles Dickens and then answer the questions that follow.**

"Oh! but he was a tight-fisted hand at the grindstone. Scrooge! a squeezing, wrenching, grasping, scraping, clutching, covetous old sinner! Hard and sharp as flint, from which no steel had ever struck out generous fire, secret, and self-contained, and solitary as an oyster. The cold within him froze his old features, nipped his pointed nose, shrivelled his cheek, stiffened his gait; made his eyes red, his thin lips blue; and spoke out shrewdly in his grating voice. A frosty rime was on his head, and on his eyebrows, and his wiry chin. He carried his own low temperature always about with him; he iced his office in the dog-days, and didn't thaw it one degree at Christmas.

External heat and cold had little influence on Scrooge. No warmth could warm, no wintry weather chill him. No wind that blew was bitterer than he, no falling snow was more intent upon its purpose, no pelting rain less open to entreaty. Foul weather didn't know where to have him. The heaviest rain, and snow, and hail, and sleet, could boast of the advantage over him in only one respect. They often "came down" handsomely, and Scrooge never did.

Nobody ever stopped him in the street to say, with gladsome looks, "My dear Scrooge, how are you? When will you come to see me?" No beggars implored him to bestow a trifle, no children asked him what it was o'clock, no man or woman ever once in all his life inquired the way to such and such a place, of Scrooge."

1. What implement mentioned in this extract is used for sharpening knives, chisels, etc.?
2. How was a spark obtained from flint?
3. Name the features of Scrooge which are mentioned.
4. What two colours are given?
5. What is the opposite word to "external"?
6. What kind of voice had Scrooge? Give another meaning to this word.
7. What is meant by the "dog-days"?
8. Give the word opposite in meaning to "thaw".
9. How did the heaviest rain, hail, snow and sleet have an advantage over Scrooge?
10. What does "trifle" mean in this passage? Give another meaning to this word.
11. What was it that children never inquired of Scrooge?
12. What did grown-up people never ask Scrooge?
13. Give the word from the extract which sounds the same as "rhyme" and state the meaning of this word when you have found it.
14. What made Scrooge walk **rather stiffly?**

23

(C) **Read this little rhyme.**

Monday's child is fair of face,
Tuesday's child is full of grace,
Wednesday's child is full of woe,
Thursday's child has far to go,
Friday's child is loving and giving,
Saturday's child works hard for its living,
And a child that's born on the Sabbath day
Is fair and wise and good and gay.

Now answer the following:—

1 Which is an 'unlucky' day to be born on?
2 Which child is generous and kind-hearted?
3 Who will probably travel a lot?
4 Which child is supposed to be good-looking?
5 Who is very hard-working?
6 On what day were you born?
7 Would you describe this rhyme as—the truth, a superstition, a fable, a parable?

8

(A) **Read the following extract from** *Modern Boys' Book of Railways* **and then answer the questions:—**

Doubters and opponents of the railways, and there were many, were still unconvinced, and though the Stockton to Darlington railway continued to function successfully in its original purpose of shifting coal, no regular passenger service had yet arrived. Just how much the steam engine did for trade is clearly illustrated by the fact that the price of coals at Darlington fell nearly ten shillings—a large sum of money in those days.

Yet there was tremendous opposition to the railways. Boys who are living in the century when man has even begun to harness atomic power for his needs can have no idea of the outcry that the arrival of the steam locomotive caused. There will always be people who oppose anything new and progressive, there will always be the timid who are fearful of things they don't understand. Added to these people were the canal owners, who realised at once how much trade from their canals the railways would steal. So the canal owners and others to whom the steam locomotive spelt disaster spread tales of what the railways would do. The peace of the countryside would be ruined, cattle would be poisoned by the foul smoke, crops damaged, hayricks set on fire by sparks from the noisy engines, all these dreadful things would happen, they prophesied.

1. What was the original purpose of the Stockton to Darlington Railway?
2. When do you think the Stockton to Darlington Railway was opened: 1588, 1603, 1825, 1905?
3. What was one of its first effects?
4. What is the latest kind of power mentioned?
5. Who were the chief opponents of the railways?
6. Why were they opposed to them?
7. Mention any two arguments put forward against the railways.
8. Who was the engineer of the Stockton to Darlington Railway—James Watt, Robert Louis Stevenson, George Stephenson?

Give one word from the extract which means the same as:—

9. An enemy.
10. To remain uncertain.
11. An engine which moves.
12. Very great.
13. Much afraid.
14. To foretell.

(B) Read this extract from *Sir Francis Drake* by James A. Williamson.

As Walsingham ushered him in, Drake beheld a woman of forty, with red-gold hair and clear complexion, steady eyes under arched brows, a thin curved nose, high cheek-bones and a long chin. She spoke in friendly familiar tones to all, yet none could mistake that she was the Queen, royal and great, more than a woman, the nation that he humbly served, or if he were a traitor, the nation that he hated. Traitors indeed often spoke with her, sometimes with murder in their minds. She knew it, but she liked to probe them. She feared nothing. She was England.

In Francis Drake she saw the best of England, the man of the sea, of bold plans and distant enterprise, the world his workshop. Drake was of middle height, sturdy and thickset, reddish of hair and beard, with round head and cheerful face, and open eyes that looked manfully on all things. Drake saw into men, though men saw but the surface of Drake, behind whose open face was a brain of the finest and a will of iron. The Queen saw all that, for they were two of a kind.

Now answer these questions:—

1 Who conducted Drake to the Queen?
2 How old was the Queen at this time?
3 Briefly describe the Queen's features.
4 What was the Queen's attitude towards traitors?
5 What words show that Drake was a good judge of men?
6 Was he tall, short, or of medium height?
7 In what way were the Queen and Drake alike?

(C) **John Bunyan (1628-1688), a tinker, wrote** *Pilgrim's Progress***, one of the world's greatest books, probably in Bedford Jail. The following extract is taken from this book. Read it and then answer the questions.**

THE HILL DIFFICULTY

I beheld then, that they all went on till they came to the foot of the hill Difficulty, at the bottom of which was a spring. There were also in the same place two other ways, besides that which came straight from the gate: one turned to the left hand, and the other to the right, at the bottom of the hill; but the narrow way lay right up the hill, and the name of the going up the side of the hill is called Difficulty. Christian went now to the spring, and drank thereof to refresh himself, and then began to go up the hill, saying,

> The hill, though high, I covet to ascend;
> The difficulty will not me offend;
> For I perceive the way to life lies here;
> Come, pluck up, heart, let's neither faint nor fear.
> Better, though difficult, the right way to go,
> Than wrong, though easy, where the end is woe.

The other two also came to the foot of the hill. But when they saw that the hill was steep and high, and that there were two other ways to go; and supposing also that these two ways might meet again with that up which Christian went, on the other side of the hill; therefore they were resolved to go in these ways. Now the name of one of those ways was Danger, and the name of the other Destruction. So the one took the way which is called Danger, which did lead him into a great wood; and the other took directly up the way to Destruction, which led him into a wide field, full of dark mountains, where he stumbled and fell, and rose no more.

1 What was there at the bottom of the hill Difficulty where people could refresh themselves?
2 How many people actually mentioned here came to the foot of the hill?
3 Who alone was not dismayed by its steepness?
4 What did he do to comfort himself when climbing the hill?
5 What kind of road was it that went right up the hill?
6 What were the other two roads called?
7 Where did they lead to?

9

(A) Read this extract from *Gulliver's Travels* by Dean Swift (1667-1745). It tells how Gulliver, after being shipwrecked, was captured by the tiny people.

I was extremely tired. I lay down on the grass, which was very short and soft, where I slept sounder than I ever remembered to have done in my life, and, as I reckoned, about nine hours; for when I awakened it was just daylight. I attempted to rise, but was not able to stir; for as I happened to lie on my back, I found my arms and legs were strongly fastened on each side to the ground; and my hair, which was long and thick, tied down in the same manner. I likewise felt several slender ligatures across my body, from my arm-pits to my thighs. I could only look upwards, the sun began to grow hot, and the light offended my eyes. I heard a confused noise about me, but, in the posture I lay, could see nothing except the sky. In a little time I felt something alive, moving on my left leg, which advancing gently forward, over my breast, came almost up to my chin; when bending my eyes downward as much as I could, I perceived it to be a human creature not six inches high, with a bow and arrow in his hands, and a quiver at his back. In the meantime, I felt at least forty more of the same kind (as I conjectured) following the first. I was in the utmost astonishment, and roared so loud, that they all ran back in a fright; and some of them, as I was afterwards told, were hurt with the falls they got by leaping from my sides upon the ground.

Answer the following:—

1 For how long did Gulliver sleep?

2 Where did he sleep?

3 What does "ligatures" mean?

4 In which direction only could Gulliver look?

5 What did he hear?

6 About how tall was the man who first climbed on Gulliver's body?

7 What did he carry?

8 How many more of them were there?

9 What did Gulliver do?

10 What was the result?

(B) Read this passage about the famous outlaw Robin Hood.

   Winter came and passed, and summer returned to clothe Sherwood in green, and Robin and his band flourished, while men said that King Richard was on his way back to England after his captivity. The outlaws hunted the deer and lived right royally, and even in the depth of winter Marian declared that she had never lived so happily as in the forest. From time to time Robin and his men made a haul from some band of Normans who passed along the forest ways, or spoiled some fat prelate of the gains he had squeezed from his unfortunate tenants, and no man dared to oppose him after the discomfiture of the Sheriff of Nottingham and his men when they went to seize the outlaw chief.
   Robin was careful that his men were kept busy over something, for he knew that idleness breeds discontent more surely than anything else. When the weather was open there was hunting in the forest, and if they were forced to keep at home in their secret glade there were bouts of arms, archery contests, and quarter-staff play, at which both Friar Tuck and Little John were mighty players, beating even Robin Hood himself, though he too was skilled with the long staff.

Answer the following:—

1   Where was "the secret glade"?
2   What was the King doing who is mentioned here?
3   What is a "prelate"?
4   What does idleness breed?
5   What official is referred to?
6   Two of Robin's men are mentioned. Who are they?
7   Who had once been captured by Robin Hood?
8   What is meant by "tenants"?
9   When the men were forced to remain in hiding, what did they do?

(C) Read this extract from *Robinson Crusoe* by Daniel Defoe. Defoe was born in London in 1661 and died in 1731. He narrowly escaped being hanged for taking part in Monmouth's rebellion and had a roving and adventurous life. He was once sentenced to stand in the pillory. *Robinson Crusoe* has been translated into many languages. It was published in 1719 and is founded on the true story of Alexander Selkirk, a ship-wrecked sailor of the time.

ROBINSON CRUSOE TAKES LEAVE OF THE ISLAND

When I took leave of this island I carried on board, for relics, the great goat-skin cap I had made, my umbrella, and one of the parrots, also I forgot not to take the money I formerly mentioned, which had lain by me so long useless that it had grown rusty or tarnished, and could hardly pass for silver, till it had been a little rubbed and handled; as also some money I found in the wreck of the Spanish ship. And thus I left the island, the 19th of December, as I found by the ship's account, in the year 1686, after I had been upon it eight-and-twenty years, two months, and nineteen days, being delivered from this second captivity the same day of the month that I first made my escape in the longboat from among the Moors of Salee. In this vessel, after a long voyage, I arrived in England the 11th of June, in the year 1687, having been thirty-five years absent.

Now answer these questions:—

1. For how long was Robinson Crusoe absent from England?
2. How long did he spend on the island?
3. What was the date on which he left the island?
4. How did he know it was on this date?
5. What was the date of his arrival in England?
6. How long did the voyage take from the island to England?
7. Mention briefly what he took with him when he left the island.
8. What did he take them for?

10

(A) Read the following gardening instructions and then answer the questions below.

SPRAYING FLUIDS

Burgundy Mixture. 1¼ lbs. washing soda is dissolved in 8 gallons of water in a wooden tub. 1 lb. copper sulphate, previously dissolved in 2 gallons of water, is then added.

Bordeaux Mixture. Dissolve 1 lb. copper sulphate in 8 gallons of water. This will take some days. 1½ lbs. quicklime is slaked with the remaining 2 gallons of water and strained into the copper sulphate solution to make 10 gallons.

Derris Powder. Use as directed, either as a wet spray, or for dusting.

Liver of Sulphur. 1 oz. to 2 gallons of water.

Nicotine Spray (poison). 1 fluid ounce pure nicotine and ½ lb. soft soap in 12 gallons of water.

Lime Sulphur. Use ready-made lime sulphur, and dilute as directed for the various purposes.

Tar Oil Winter Wash. Dilute with water 1 part neat fluid to 12-14 parts water.

1 Which of these sprays is used in the winter?
2 What substance which is used as a spray is found in tobacco?
3 Which wash is largely a by-product of coal?
4 Which insecticide can be applied either in a wet or dry form?
5 Which spray is poison?
6 Which of these spraying fluids contains the names of towns?
7 What do you think "slaked" means here?

(B) John Buchan, later Lord Tweedsmuir, was born in Perth in Scotland in 1875 and died in 1940. He wrote many interesting adventure stories such as *The Thirty-nine Steps, Prester John, Greenmantle, Huntingtower, Mr. Standfast, The Path of the King, Salute to Adventurers,* and others well-known to schools. His "heroes" include Richard Hannay, Blenkiron, and Peter Pienaar, and his "villains", Laputa, Constantine Karolides and Von Stumn.

John Buchan had a most distinguished career. He served in France with the British Army during the First World War, was a Member of Parliament from 1927 to 1935, and Governor-General of Canada from 1936 until his death.

The following extract is taken from *Greenmantle*, an exciting story of the First World War. Read it and then answer the questions that follow.

HANNAY IN HIDING

That night I realised the crazy folly of war. When I saw the splintered shell of Ypres and heard hideous tales of German doings, I used to want to see the whole land of the Boche given up to fire and sword. I thought we could never end the war properly without giving the Huns some of their own medicine. But that woodcutter's cottage cured me of such nightmares. I was for punishing the guilty but letting the innocent go free. It was our business to thank God and keep our hands clean from the ugly blunders to which Germany's madness had driven her. What good would it do Christian folk to burn little huts like this and leave children's bodies by the wayside? To be able to laugh and to be merciful are the only things that make man better than the beasts.

The place, as I have said, was desperately poor. The woman's face had the skin stretched tight over the bones and that transparency which means underfeeding; I fancied she did not have the liberal allowance that soldiers' wives get in England. The children looked better nourished but it was by their mother's sacrifice. I did my best to cheer them up. I told them long yarns about Africa and lions and tigers, and I got pieces of wood and whittled them into toys. I am fairly good with a knife, and I carved very presentable likenesses of a monkey, a springbok, and a rhinoceros. The children went to bed hugging the first toys, I expect, they ever possessed.

1 Whom did John Buchan later become known as?
2 What important official position did he hold?
3 What nationality was he?
4 What briefly did the speaker think about war?

5   What is meant here by a "splintered shell"?
6   What two words in this passage are used to denote Germans?
7   Where did the speaker hide?
8   What two things make men better than beasts?
9   Why did Hannay think that the woman suffered from under-feeding?
10 What did the woman do in order that the children should not go hungry?
11 In what other country had the speaker been?
12 What did he do to amuse the children?

(C) Read this extract from *The Four Feathers* by A. E. W. Mason.

HARRY FEVERSHAM RECEIVES THE WHITE FEATHERS

"The post is in," she said. "There are letters, one, two, three for you, and a little box."

She held the box out to him as she spoke, a little white jeweller's cardboard box, and was at once struck by its absence of weight.

"It must be empty," she said.

Yet it was most carefully sealed and tied. Feversham broke the seals and unfastened the string. He looked at the address. The box had been forwarded from his lodgings, and he was not familiar with the handwriting.

"There is some mistake," he said as he shook the lid open; and then he stopped abruptly. Three white feathers fluttered out of the box, swayed and rocked for a moment in the air, and then, one after another, settled gently down upon the floor. They lay like flakes of snow upon the dark polished boards. But they were not whiter than Harry Feversham's cheeks. He stood and stared at the feathers until he felt a light touch upon his arm. He looked and saw Ethne's gloved hand upon his sleeve.

"What does it mean?" she asked. There was some perplexity in her voice, but nothing more than perplexity. The smile upon her face and the loyal confidence of her eyes showed she had never a doubt that his first word would lift it from her. "What does it mean?"

Now answer these questions:—

1 What was meant by sending white feathers to Harry Feversham?
2 How many were there?
3 How many letters were received by Harry?
4 What struck Ethne about the box?
5 What did the feathers look like?
6 What did Harry look like when he saw the feathers?
7 What were Ethne's feelings towards Harry?

11

(A) Read this extract about Shylock the Jew, a character in Shakespeare's *Merchant of Venice*. It is taken from Lamb's *Tales from Shakespeare*.

Shylock the Jew lived at Venice; he was an usurer, who had amassed an immense fortune by lending money at great interest to Christian merchants. Shylock, being a hard-hearted man, exacted the payment of the money he lent with such severity that he was much disliked by all good men, and particularly by Antonio, a young merchant of Venice; and Shylock as much hated Antonio, because he used to lend money to people in distress, and would never take any interest for the money he lent; therefore there was great enmity between this covetous Jew and the generous merchant Antonio. Whenever Antonio met Shylock on the Rialto (or Exchange), he used to reproach him with his usuries and hard dealings, which the Jew would bear with seeming patience, while he secretly meditated revenge.

Now answer these questions:—

1 Where did Shylock live?
2 How had he made a great fortune?
3 What sort of man was he?
4 Who particularly disliked Shylock?
5 Why did Shylock also dislike him?

6 What was the place called in Venice where merchants met for business?
7 What is a similar place called in London?
8 What did Antonio reproach Shylock with?
9 Name words from the passage which mean
   (a) greedy or grasping, (b) bitterness, (c) thought about in secret, (d) collected together.

(B) Pompeii and Herculaneum were two Roman cities buried in molten lava from an eruption by the volcano Vesuvius near Naples in 79 A.D. Lord Lytton wrote a book about it in 1834 when the first edition was published called *The Last Days of Pompeii*. The following extract is taken from this book.

> Facing the steps of the Temple of Jupiter, with folded arms, and a knit and contemptuous brow, stood a man of about fifty years of age. His dress was remarkably plain—not so much from its material, as from the absence of all those ornaments which were worn by the Pompeians of every rank—partly from the love of show, partly, also, because they were chiefly wrought into those shapes deemed most efficacious in resisting the assaults of magic and the influence of the evil eye. His forehead was high and bald; the few locks that remained at the back of his head were concealed by a sort of cowl, which made a part of his cloak, to be raised or lowered at pleasure, and was now drawn half-way over the head, as a protection from the rays of the sun. The colour of his garments was brown, no popular hue with the Pompeians; all the usual admixtures of scarlet or purple seemed carefully excluded. His belt, or girdle, contained a small receptacle for ink, which hooked on to the girdle, a stilus (or implement of writing), and tablets of no ordinary size. What was rather remarkable, the cincture held no purse, which was the almost indispensable appurtenance of the girdle, even when that purse had the misfortune to be empty.

Now answer these questions:—

1 What is "lava"?
2 What heathen god is mentioned?

3 About what age was the person described here?
4 How was he dressed?
5 What kind of forehead had he?
6 What kind of colour was unpopular with the Pompeians?
7 What articles were attached to his belt or girdle?
8 One object was missing. What was it?
9 What is meant by "brow" here? Give another meaning of this word.
10 How did the Pompeians usually dress?

(C) **Read this extract.**

A COUNTRY GENTLEMAN

Will Wimble is younger brother to a baronet, and descended of the ancient family of the Wimbles. He is now between forty and fifty; but being bred to no business and born to no estate, he generally lives with his elder brother as superintendent of his game. He hunts a pack of dogs better than any man in the country, and is very famous for finding out a hare. He is extremely well versed in all the little handicrafts of an idle man. He makes a May-fly to a miracle: and furnishes the whole country with angle-rods. As he is a good-natured officious fellow, and very much esteemed upon account of his family, he is a welcome guest at every house, and keeps up a good correspondence among all the gentlemen about him. He carries a tulip-root in his pocket from one to another, or exchanges a puppy between a couple of friends that live perhaps in the opposite sides of the county.

Will is a particular favourite of all the young heirs, whom he frequently obliges with a net that he has weaved, or a setting-dog that he has made himself: he now and then presents small gifts to their mothers or sisters. These gentleman-like manufactures and obliging little humours, make Will the darling of his country.

Joseph Addison (1672-1719).

Answer the following:—

1 About what age was Will Wimble?
2 With whom did he generally live, and in what capacity?
3 What did he do better than anyone else?
4 Why was he much esteemed?
5 What is meant by, "He makes a May-fly to a miracle?"
6 What did he often exchange?
7 With whom was he a particular favourite?
8 What is meant by "born to no estate"?

12

(A) Read this extract from *The Natural History of Selborne* **by Gilbert White, and then answer the questions that follow.**

There is a wonderful spirit of sociality in the brute creation. Many horses, though quiet with company, will not stay one minute in a field by themselves: the strongest fences cannot restrain them. My neighbour's horse will not only not stay by himself abroad, but he will not bear to be left alone in a strange stable without discovering the utmost impatience, and endeavouring to break the rack and manger with his fore-feet. He has been known to leap out of a stable window after company; and yet in other respects is remarkably quiet, but will neglect the finest pasture that is not recommended by society. It would be needless to instance sheep, which constantly flock together.

But this propensity seems not to be confined to animals of the same species; for we know a doe, still alive, that was brought up from a little fawn with a dairy of cows; with them it goes a-field, and with them it returns to the yard. The dogs of the house take no notice of this deer, being used to her; but if strange dogs come by, a chase ensues; while the master smiles to see his favourite securely leading her pursuers over hedge, or gate, or stile; till she returns to the cows, who, with fierce lowings and menacing horns, drive the assailants quite out of the pasture.

1. What is meant by "brute creation"?
2. What is it that many horses are unable to do?
3. What has one particular horse been known to do when left alone?
4. What other animals mentioned dislike being alone?
5. What is a fawn?
6. Who did the doe follow to pasture?
7. What happened when strange dogs met the doe?
8. Give words from the passage which mean the same as,
    (a) tendency, (b) class or group, (c) threatening, (d) attackers.
9. What do you think is meant by,
    (a) rack and manger? (b) fierce lowings? (c) a chase ensues?

(B)
UPON WESTMINSTER BRIDGE, by William Wordsworth. September 3, 1802.

Read this well-known poem and then try and answer the questions.

Earth has not anything to show more fair:
Dull would he be of soul who could pass by
A sight so touching in its majesty:
This City now doth like a garment wear

The beauty of the morning: silent, bare,
Ships, towers, domes, theatres, and temples lie
Open unto the fields, and to the sky,
All bright and glittering in the smokeless air.

Never did sun more beautifully steep
In his first splendour, valley, rock, or hill;
Ne'er saw I, never felt, a calm so deep!
The river glideth at his own sweet will:
Dear God! the very houses seem asleep;
And all that mighty heart is lying still!

1 To what does "This City" refer?
2 During which part of the day is the bridge described?
3 What well-known 'tower' and dome would be seen from the bridge?
4 How do you know that there was more open country to be seen?
5 What kind of air was there?
6 What particularly impressed the poet about
    (a) the houses?
    (b) the river?
7 What do you think is meant by the line,
    "Never did sun more beautifully steep"?

(C) **The following passage is taken from** *The Confessions of an Opium-Eater* **by Thomas de Quincey (1785-1859).**

I left the lodgings at the same hour; and this turned out a very unfortunate occurrence for me: because, living henceforward at inns, I was drained of my money very rapidly. In a fortnight I was reduced to short allowance; that is, I could allow myself only one meal a day. From the keen appetite produced by constant exercise and mountain air acting on a youthful stomach, I soon began to suffer greatly on this slender regimen; for the single meal which I could venture to order was coffee or tea. Even this, however, was at length withdrawn: and afterwards, so long as I remained in Wales, I subsisted either on blackberries, hips, haws, etc., or on the casual hospitalities which I now and then received, in return for such little services as I had an opportunity of rendering. Sometimes I wrote letters of business for cottagers, who happened to have relatives in Liverpool, or in London: more often I wrote love-letters to their sweethearts for young women who had lived as servants in Shrewsbury, or other towns on the English border. On all such occasions I gave great satisfaction to my humble friends, and was generally treated with hospitality.

Now answer these questions:—

1 Why did it prove unfortunate to the writer when he left his lodgings?

2 How many meals a day did he allow himself?
3 Of what did these meals largely consist?
4 What did he live on when he had no money left?
5 What did he do to try and earn money or a meal?
6 How was he generally treated?
7 To what country does he refer?
8 What border town is mentioned?
9 What is meant by,
   (a) regimen? (b) casual? (c) hospitality?

13

(A)

OLIVER ASKS FOR MORE

Read this extract from that well-known book *Oliver Twist* by Charles Dickens (1812-1870).

The evening arrived; the boys took their places. The master, in his cook's uniform, stationed himself at the copper; his pauper assistants ranged themselves behind him; the gruel was served out; and a long grace was said over the short commons. The gruel disappeared; the boys whispered to each other, and winked at Oliver; while his next neighbours nudged him. Child as he was, he was desperate with hunger, and reckless with misery. He rose from the table; and advancing to the master, basin and spoon in hand, said, somewhat alarmed at his own temerity:

"Please, sir, I want some more."

The master was a fat, healthy man; but he turned very pale. He gazed in stupefied astonishment on the small rebel for some seconds, and then clung for support to the copper. The assistants were paralysed with wonder; the boys with fear.

"What!" said the master at length, in a faint voice.

"Please, sir," replied Oliver, "I want some more."

The master aimed a blow at Oliver's head with the ladle; pinioned him in his arms; and shrieked aloud for the beadle.

The board were sitting in solemn conclave, when Mr. Bumble

rushed into the room in great excitement, and addressing the gentleman in the high chair, said,

"Mr. Limbkins, I beg your pardon sir, Oliver Twist has asked for more!"

There was a general start. Horror was depicted on every countenance. "For *more!*" said Mr. Limbkins. "Compose yourself, Bumble, and answer me distinct. Do I understand that he has asked for more, after he had eaten the supper allotted by the dietary?"

"He did, sir," replied Bumble.

"That boy will be hung," said the gentleman in the white waistcoat. "I know that boy will be hung."

Now answer the following:—

1 Where did the master of the workhouse station himself?
2 What did the paupers have to eat?
3 What was said before they ate it?
4 What words in the passage indicate that there was very little of it?
5 How did Oliver show his temerity?
6 What sort of man was the master?
7 Mention the words in the passage which mean
    (a) A kind of meeting.
    (b) Fastened in one's arms.
    (c) The food allotted for the day.
8 What did the gentleman in the white waistcoat prophesy?
9 What was depicted on the faces of every member of the Board?
10 What did the master wear?

(B) Read this description of a pretty girl, HETTY, the dairymaid, from the novel *Adam Bede*, by George Eliot (1819-1880). Her real name was Mary Ann Evans. "George Eliot" was her *nom de plume.*

It is of little use for me to tell you that Hetty's cheek was like a rose-petal, that dimples played about her pouting lips, that her large dark eyes hid a soft roguishness under their long lashes, and that her curly hair, though all pushed back under her round cap while she was at work, stole back in dark delicate rings on her forehead, and about her white shell-like ears. It is of little use for me to say how lovely was the contour of her pink-and-white neckerchief tucked into her low plum-coloured stuff bodice; or how the linen butter-making apron, with its bib, seemed a thing to be imitated in silk by duchesses, since it fell in such charming lines; or how her brown stockings and thick-soled buckled shoes lost all that clumsiness which they must certainly have had when empty of her foot and ankle—of little use, unless you have seen a woman who affected you as Hetty affected her beholders; for otherwise, though you might conjure up the image of a lovely woman, she would not in the least resemble that distracting kitten-like maiden.

Now answer these questions:—

1 In this description of Hetty there is no mention of what most modern girls would use to improve their appearance. What is it?
2 What did Hetty's cheek resemble?
3 What kind of eyes did she have?
4 Why was her curly hair not seen to advantage while she was at work?
5 What other word could be used instead of "contour"?
6 In what connection is "contour" usually used?
7 What kind of apron did Hetty wear and for what purpose did she wear it?
8 What phrase in the passage means, "to imagine the figure of"?
9 What did Hetty resemble?

(C) **Read Æsop's fable** *The Lion and the Mouse* **and then attempt the questions that follow.**

A Lion was sleeping in his lair, when a Mouse, not knowing where he was going, ran over the mighty beast's nose and wakened him. The Lion clapped his paw upon the frightened little creature, and was about to make an end of him in a moment, when the Mouse, in pitiable tone, besought him to spare one who had so unconsciously offended, and not stain his honourable paws with so insignificant a prey. The Lion, smiling at his little prisoner's fright, generously let him go. Now it happened no long time after, that the Lion, while ranging the woods for his prey, fell into the toils of the hunters; and finding himself entangled without hope of escape, set up a roar that filled the whole forest with its echo. The Mouse, recognising the voice of his former preserver, ran to the spot, and without more ado set to work to nibble the knot in the cord that bound the Lion, and in a short time set the noble beast at liberty; thus convincing him that kindness is seldom thrown away, and that there is no creature so much below another but that he may have it in his power to return a good office.

1 Where was the lion sleeping?
2 How did the mouse awaken the lion?
3 Give a word in the passage which means
   (a) "Not knowing what one is doing".
   (b) "Very unimportant".
4 What was the lion doing not long after he had let the mouse go?
5 What happened to the lion?
6 When he found that there was no hope of escape, what did he do?
7 What kind of trap was the lion caught in?
8 What did the mouse do to help his friend?
9 What would you say in simple language is the moral of this fable?

14

(A) **Read this extract from** *The Children's Life of the Bee*, **by Maurice Maeterlinck, and then answer the questions below.**

There is no doubt that if some person, who neither knows nor respects the habits of the bee, were suddenly to fling open the hive, this would turn itself immediately into a burning-bush of heroism and fury; but the slight amount of skill needed to deal with the matter can be readily acquired. Let but a little smoke be deftly applied, let us be gentle and careful in our movements, and the heavily-armed workers will permit themselves to be robbed without the least thought of using their sting. It is not the fact, as some people have stated, that the bees recognize their owner, nor have they any fear of man; but, when the smoke reaches them, when they become aware of what is happening, so quietly and without any haste or disturbance, they imagine that this is not the attack of an enemy against whom any defence is possible, but that it is some natural catastrophe, to which they will do well to submit. Instead of vainly struggling, therefore, their one thought is to safeguard their future; and they rush at once to their reserves of honey, into which they eagerly plunge themselves in order to possess the material for starting a new city immediately, no matter where, should the old one be destroyed or they compelled to abandon it.

1 If a person tried suddenly to open a hive, what would happen?
2 What precaution should a person take when he opens a hive?
3 What do the bees imagine this is?
4 What do they at once do?
5 Why do they do this?
6 What is meant by,
    (a) Deftly?
    (b) Catastrophe?
    (c) Abandon?

(B) Mrs. Gaskell (1810-1865) wrote a delightful picture of village life in her novel *Cranford* which is really a Cheshire village named Knutsford. This village remains much the same today as when Mrs. Gaskell wrote about it about one hundred years ago. The following extract is about Miss Betsy Barker's Alderney cow.

    An old lady had an Alderney cow, which she looked upon as a daughter. You could not pay the short quarter of an hour call without being told of the wonderful milk or wonderful intelligence of this animal. The whole town knew and kindly regarded Miss Betsy's Alderney; therefore great was the sympathy and regret when, in an unguarded moment, the poor cow tumbled into a lime pit. She moaned so loudly that she was soon heard and rescued; but meanwhile the poor beast had lost most of her hair, and came out looking naked, cold and miserable in a bare skin. Everybody pitied the animal, though a few could not restrain their smiles at her droll appearance. Miss Betsy Barker absolutely cried with sorrow and dismay, and it was said she thought of trying a bath of oil.

Now answer these questions.

1 What did Miss Barker talk about if anyone called on her?
2 Why did the cow lose her hair?
3 What remedy did Miss Barker think of applying?
4 Why were a few people amused after the accident to the cow?

Write TRUE, NOT TRUE, or IT IS IMPOSSIBLE TO TELL, about each of the three following statements:—

5 The poor cow lost its way.
6 Miss Barker was very proud of her Alderney cow.
7 Everybody was very amused at the accident to the cow.
8 Do you know where Alderney is?

(C) **Mr. H. G. Wells was born on 21 September 1866 at Bromley in Kent, and died in London on 13 August 1946. He has written, among a great many other things, a series of scientific romances.** *The Invisible Man,* **from which the following passage is taken, was written in 1897.**

I resolved to explore the house, and spent some time in doing so as noiselessly as possible. The house was very old and tumble-down, damp, so that the paper in the attics was peeling from the walls, and rat-infested. Most of the door handles were stiff, and I was afraid to turn them. Several rooms I did inspect were unfurnished, and others were littered with theatrical lumber, bought secondhand, I judged from its appearance. In one room next to his I found a lot of old clothes. I began routing among these, and in my eagerness forgot again the evident sharpness of his ears. I heard a stealthy footstep, and, looking up just in time, saw him peeping in at the tumbled heap and holding an old-fashioned revolver in his hand. I stood perfectly still while he stared about open-mouthed and suspicious.

1 Why was the writer afraid to turn the door handles?
2 What did the writer find in the house?
3 What was the condition of the house?
4 What had made the man with the revolver suspicious?
5 What kind of revolver was it?
6 What do you think is meant by
 (a) Theatrical lumber?
 (b) Routing?
 (c) Rat-infested.

Write TRUE, NOT TRUE, or IT IS IMPOSSIBLE TO TELL, about each of the following statements:—

7 The man with the revolver lived in the house
8 The house was completely furnished.
9 The man with the revolver had good hearing.
10 The writer was a burglar.

15

(A) Read the following extract about *Lumbering in Canada* and then answer the questions that follow.

The present output of Eastern Canada consists mainly of spruce and balsam firs, whose logs provide excellent material for the pulp and paper industries.

In some of the more accessible districts timber is now felled throughout the year, but the main lumbering season is in winter, for the frozen state of the ground facilitates transport, making it easy for the logs to be hauled, by horse-drawn sledges or motor tractors, to the nearest shoot, down which they slide to the banks of a stream to await the spring thaw. The lakes act as collecting basins where logs are assembled before being floated farther down stream to the saw-, pulp- and paper-mills, whose machinery is driven by electric power.

For centuries hunting animals for furs has been a winter occupation in the forests. Much trapping is still carried on, and there are also fur farms, where animals are reared for their skins. Montreal, Winnipeg, and Edmonton, together with New York, St. Louis, and London, are the world's leading fur markets.

1 What is the timber of Eastern Canada largely used for?
2 Why do you think the main lumbering season is in the winter?
3 What kind of power is supplied to the saw, pulp, and paper mills?
4 From where do you think this power is obtained?
5 Can you name any of the Great Lakes?
6 What has been a winter occupation in the forests for a long time?
7 What are the world's leading fur markets?

(B) **Read the following extract about LISTER from a modern science book and then answer the questions.**

While Pasteur was carrying out his researches on bacteria, an English surgeon named Joseph Lister was worrying about the high death-rate resulting from surgical operations. Very often the operation wound refused to heal; it festered, that is, it became septic. Blood poisoning then followed and frequently the patient died.

When he heard about Pasteur's discoveries, Lister wondered if bacteria could be the cause of festering. He put his theory to the test. All the instruments which he used in his hospital were, before use, dipped in carbolic acid. Bandages were treated in the same way. The hands of the surgeon and of the nurses were well washed with the liquid.

As a result of these precautions, deaths from blood poisoning after operations became much less frequent. Other hospitals followed Lister's example and anti-septic surgery became widely practised.

Joseph Lister, who later became Lord Lister, showed that festering and blood poisoning could be prevented by killing the bacteria which caused them. Nowadays other anti-septic liquids are used and other methods of sterilising surgical instruments and dressings. Bacteria can be killed by heating, as you know. Instruments and dressings are therefore either dipped in boiling water or kept in hot ovens.

1. What did Lister find often resulted from surgical operations?
2. What did Lister wonder was the cause of wounds festering?
3. What liquid did he use to test his theory?
4. What was placed in the liquid?
5. What were the results of Lister's precautions?
6. What was the name given to this new kind of surgery?
7. Can you name any other anti-septic fluids which are now in use?
8. What is another way of killing bacteria?
9. What two words can be used for the 'killing of bacteria'?
10. Who first carried out research on bacteria?

(C) **Read this extract from** *Eothen*, **a well-known travel book, by A. W. Kinglake.**

The camel kneels to receive her load, and for a while she will allow the packing to go on with silent resignation; but when she begins to suspect that her master is putting more than a just burden upon her poor hump, she turns round her supple neck, and looks sadly upon the increasing load, and then gently remonstrates against the wrong with the sigh of a patient wife. If sighs will not move you, she can weep. You soon learn to pity and soon to love her for the sake of her gentle and womanish ways.

You cannot, of course, put an English or any other riding

saddle upon the back of the camel, but your quilt or carpet, or whatever you carry for the purpose of lying on at night, is folded and fastened on to the pack-saddle upon the top of the hump, and on this you ride, or rather sit. You sit as a man sits on a chair when he sits astride. I made an improvement on this plan: I had my English stirrups strapped on to the crossbars of the pack-saddle; and thus, by gaining rest for my dangling legs, and gaining, too, the power of varying my position more easily than I could otherwise have done, I added very much to my comfort.

Now answer these questions:—

1 In what position does the camel receive her load?
2 For a while how does she allow the packing to go on?
3 What does she do when she suspects that she is over-loaded?
4 What does the traveller use in addition to ride on the camel?
5 How did the traveller add to his comfort in this respect?
6 What is the NOUN formed from the verb 'to suspect'?
7 What is the VERB formed from the noun 'resignation'?
8 Give the opposite word to 'patient'.
9 What part of speech is
    (a) Gently?
    (b) Gentle?
10 What word in the passage means 'to protest against'?

16

(A) **Read the following extract from *Lavengro*, written by George Borrow in the year 1851.**

One day it happened that, being on my rambles, I entered a green lane which I had never seen before; at first it was rather narrow, but as I advanced it became considerably wider; in the middle was a drift-way with deep ruts, but right and left was a space carpeted with a sward of trefoil and clover; there was no lack of trees, chiefly ancient oaks, which, flinging out their arms from either side, nearly formed a canopy, and afforded a pleasant shelter from the rays of the sun, which was burning fiercely above. Suddenly a group of objects attracted my attention. Beneath one of the largest of the trees upon the grass was a kind of low tent or booth, from the top of which a thin smoke was curling; beside it stood a couple of light carts, whilst two or three lean horses or ponies were cropping the herbage which was growing nigh. Wondering to whom this odd tent could belong, I advanced till I was close before it, when I found that it consisted of two tilts, like those of waggons, placed upon the ground fronting each other, connected behind by a sail or large piece of canvas which was but partially drawn across the top; upon the ground in the intervening space, was a fire, over which, supported by a kind of iron crowbar, hung a cauldron.

Now answer the following:—

1 What do you suppose the writer was doing in the first place?
2 What kind of lane was it?
3 What were the chief kind of trees growing in the lane?
4 How did they afford shelter from the sun?
5 What did the writer see beneath one of the largest of the trees?
6 What was coming from the top of this object?
7 What stood beside it?
8 What word in the passage suggests
   (a) Grass? (b) A kind of cooking utensil? (c) Horses "feeding upon"?
9 Give the word opposite in meaning to
   (a) Advanced, (b) Beneath, (c) Deep, (d) Fiercely.

(B) Read this extract from *The Tower of London*, by a famous historical novelist, William Harrison Ainsworth, who was born in Manchester in 1805 and died at Reigate in 1882.

Mary made her public entry into the city of London on the 3rd of August, 1553. The most magnificent preparations were made for her arrival, and as the procession of the usurper—for such Jane was now universally styled—to the Tower had been remarkable for pomp and splendour, it was determined, on the present occasion, to surpass it. The queen's entrance was arranged to take place at Aldgate, and the streets along which she was to pass were covered with fine gravel from thence to the Tower, and railed on either side. Within the rails stood the crafts of the city in the dresses of their order; and at certain intervals were stationed the officers of the guard and their attendants, arrayed in velvet and silk, and having long staves in their hands to keep off the crowd. Hung with rich arras, tapestry, carpets, and, in some instances, with cloths of tissue gold and velvet, the houses presented a gorgeous appearance. Every window was filled with richly-attired dames, while the roofs, walls, gables, and steeples, were crowded with curious spectators.

Can you answer the following?

1 What kind of preparations were made for Mary's entry into the city of London?
2 Where was the queen to enter the city?
3 What was peculiar about the streets?
4 Who was the usurper?
5 What do you think is meant by "the crafts of the city"?
6 Who were arrayed in velvet and silk?
7 Where did the queen's procession end?
8 What parts of the houses were crowded with curious spectators?
9 What words in the passage could be used to fill in the following?
    (a) Great ---------- were made for the procession.
    (b) The officers had long --------- to keep back the crowd.
    (c) The windows were filled with ------ ------ ladies.
10 What word in the extract means 'one who wrongfully seizes the throne'?

(C) **THE ARMADA SETS SAIL FOR ENGLAND IN 1588.** From *The History of England*, by J. A. Froude.

Read this extract about a famous event in English history and then answer the questions that follow.

The scene as the fleet passed out of the harbour must have been singularly beautiful. It was a treacherous interval of real summer. The early sun was lighting the long chain of the Gallician mountains, marking with shadows the cleft defiles and shining softly on the white walls and vineyards of Corunna. The wind was light and falling towards a calm; the great galleons drifted slowly with the tide on the purple water, the long streamers trailing from the trucks, the red crosses, the emblem of the crusade, showing bright upon the hanging sails. The fruit boats were bringing off the last fresh supplies, and the pinnaces hastening to the ships with the last loiterers on shore. Out of thirty thousand men who that morning stood upon the decks of the proud Armada, twenty thousand and more were never again to see the hills of Spain. Of the remnant who in two short months crept back ragged and torn, all but a few hundred returned to die.

1 How did the fleet appear as it passed out of harbour?
2 Which harbour do you think is meant here?
3 What probable time of year was it?
4 What were the ships called?
5 How were they decorated?
6 What were the small boats called?
7 How many men comprised the Armada?
8 About how many would never see the hills of Spain again?
9 What words in this extract mean
    (a) People who linger?
    (b) A time in between?
    (c) Those who remain?

17

(A) ELEGY WRITTEN IN A COUNTRY CHURCH-YARD, by Thomas Gray (1716-1771).

Read the first four verses from this well-known poem and then try and answer the questions that follow.

> The curfew tolls the knell of parting day,
> The lowing herd winds slowly o'er the lea,
> The ploughman homeward plods his weary way,
> And leaves the world to darkness and to me.
>
> Now fades the glimmering landscape on the sight,
> And all the air a solemn stillness holds,
> Save where the beetle wheels his droning flight,
> And drowsy tinklings lull the distant folds:
>
> Save that from yonder ivy-mantled tower
> The moping owl does to the moon complain
> Of such as, wandering near her secret bower,
> Molest her ancient solitary reign.
>
> Beneath those rugged elms, that yew tree's shade
> Where heaves the turf in many a mouldering heap,
> Each in his narrow cell for ever laid,
> The rude Forefathers of the hamlet sleep.

1 What was the 'curfew'?
2 What word do you think means 'field'?
3 Which line in the poem suggests a tired workman?
4 Name (a) a bird, (b) an insect, and (c) two animals suggested in the poem.
5 How is dusk best described?
6 How is the owl described?
7 Where were the ancestors of the villagers buried?
8 Where did the owl live?

(B) Read the following extract from *Westward Ho!* written in 1855 by Charles Kingsley (1819-1875).

One more glance at the golden tropic sea, and the golden tropic evenings by the shore of New Granada, in the golden Spanish Main.

The bay of Santa Martha is rippling before the land-breeze, one sheet of living flame. The mighty forests are sparkling with myriad fire-flies. The lazy mist which lounges round the inner hills shines golden in the sunset rays; and, nineteen thousand feet aloft, the mighty peak of Horqueta cleaves the abyss of air, rose red against the dark blue vault of heaven. The rosy cone fades to a dull leaden hue; but only for a while. The stars flash out one by one, and Venus, like another moon, tinges the eastern snows with gold, and sheds across the bay a long yellow line of rippling light. Everywhere is glory and richness. What wonder if the earth in that enchanted land be as rich to her inmost depths as she is upon the surface? The heaven, the hills, the sea, are one sparkling garland of jewels—what wonder if the soil be jewelled also? if every watercourse and bank of earth be spangled with emeralds and rubies, with grains of gold, and feathered wreaths of native silver?

Now answer these questions:—

1 What do you understand by "Spanish Main"?
2 How is the bay of Santa Martha described?
3 Give another word which could be used instead of 'myriad'.
4 How high was the peak of Horqueta?
5 Name a planet mentioned.
6 What is likened to a 'garland of jewels'?
7 What two gems are mentioned?
8 Two precious metals are referred to. What are they?
9 From the passage find the word which means most nearly the same as
    (a) Peak (b) Abyss (c) Earth (d) Leaden (e) Coloured.

(C) This extract is from an abridged edition of *Masterman Ready* written in 1841 by Captain Frederick Marryat (1792-1848).

It was in the month of October, 18 - -, that the *Pacific*, a large ship, was running before a heavy gale of wind in the middle of the vast Atlantic Ocean. She had but little sail, for the wind was so strong that the canvas would have been split into pieces by the furious blasts before which she was driven through the waves, which were very high, and following her almost as fast as she darted through their boiling waters; sometimes heaving up her stern and sinking her bows down so deep into the hollow of the sea that it appeared as if she would have dived down underneath the waves; but she was a fine vessel, and the captain was a good seaman, who did what he considered best for the safety of his vessel, and then put his trust in that Providence who is ever watchful over us.

The captain stood before the wheel, watching the men who were steering the ship; for when you are running before a heavy gale it requires great attention to the helm: and as he looked around him and up at the heavens, he sung in a low voice the words of a sea-song:
 'One wide water all around us,
 All above us one black sky.'

Answer the following:—

1 Where was the *Pacific* at sea?
2 What type of vessel was it?
3 What kind of weather did she encounter?
4 In what part of the ship are the bows?
5 In what part of the ship is the stern?
6 What sort of man was the captain?
7 What is personified here, that is, addressed as if it were a living person?
8 Where did the captain stand?
9 Why did he watch the men who were steering the ship?
10 In what way does the song indicate the weather they were having?
11 There is a word *pronounced the same*, but *spelt differently* for each of the following. Can you give the word?
 (a) Weather (b) Canvas (c) Sail (d) Which.

18

(A) Read the following passage from *Alice Through the Looking Glass*, by Lewis Carroll.

'Tickets please!' said the Guard, putting his head in at the window. In a moment everybody was holding out a ticket: they were about the same size as the people, and quite seemed to fill the carriage.
'Now then! Show your ticket, child!' the Guard went on, looking angrily at Alice. And a great many voices all said together ('like the chorus of a song,' thought Alice), 'Don't keep him waiting, child! Why, his time is worth a thousand pounds a minute!'
'I'm afraid I haven't got one,' Alice said in a frightened tone: 'there wasn't a ticket-office where I came from.' And again the chorus of voices went on. 'There wasn't room for one where she came from. The land there is worth a thousand pounds an inch!'
'Don't make excuses,' said the Guard: 'you should have bought one from the engine-driver.' And once more the chorus of voices went on with 'The man that drives the engine. Why the smoke alone is worth a thousand pounds a puff!'
Alice thought to herself, 'Then there's no use in speaking.' The voices didn't join in this time, as she hadn't spoken, but, to her great surprise, they all *thought* in chorus (I hope you understand what *thinking in chorus* means—for I must confess that I don't), 'Better say nothing at all. Language is worth a thousand pounds a word!'
'I shall dream about a thousand pounds tonight, I know I shall!' thought Alice.
All this time the Guard was looking at her, first through a telescope, then through a microscope, and then through an opera-glass. At last he said, 'You're travelling the wrong way,' and shut up the window and went away.

Now answer the following:—

1 What was Alice doing at this time?
2 Give any three examples of exaggerated speech used in this passage.
3 Why did Alice think that she would dream of a thousand pounds?

4 What objects are used for surveying things at a distance?
5 What instrument magnifies things?
6 What did the Guard ask Alice for?
7 What rather unusual suggestion did the Guard make to Alice?
8 What was peculiar about the tickets?
9 Write in full the meaning of the following:—
    (a) haven't (b) wasn't (c) don't (d) I'm.
10 Write the shortened form of
    (a) There is (b) did not (c) had not (d) you are.

(B) Read the following passage from *Old St. Paul's*, by W. H. Ainsworth, and then answer the questions.

> London now presented a lamentable spectacle. Not a street but had a house in it marked with a red cross—some streets had many such. The bells were continually tolling for burials, and the dead-carts went their melancholy rounds at night and were constantly loaded. Fresh directions were issued by the authorities; and as domestic animals were considered to be a medium of conveying the infection, an order, which was immediately carried into effect, was given to destroy all dogs and cats. But this plan proved prejudicial rather than the reverse, as the bodies of the poor animals, most of which were drowned in the Thames, being washed ashore, produced a horrible and noxious effluvium, supposed to contribute materially to the propagation of the distemper.

1 How were many houses marked?
2 Who once wore this emblem on their armour?
3 What gave the sign for burials?
4 What were 'dead-carts'?
5 What animals were thought to spread the disease?
6 What was ordered to be done with them?
7 Why was it a bad plan?

8 Give another totally different meaning of the word 'distemper'.
9 What is usually the opposite word to 'reverse' when applied to coins?
10 Give words from the passage which mean,
   (a) disease (b) sad (c) harmful (d) smell.

(C) **The following extract is from** Hereward the Wake, **by Charles Kingsley. Read it carefully and see if you can answer the questions.**

"Pluck out the English hog's hair and beard, and put him blindfold in the midst of his pots, and see what a smash we shall have."

Hereward pretended not to understand the words, which were spoken in French; but when they were interpreted to him, he grew somewhat red about the beard.

Submit he would not. But if he defended himself, and made an uproar in the king's Court, he might very likely find himself riding Odin's horse before the hour was out. However, for him, the wine and beer had made him stout of heart, and happily when one fellow laid hold of his beard, he resisted sturdily.

The man struck him, and that hard. Hereward, hot of temper, and careless of life, struck him again, right under the ear.

The fellow dropped for dead.

Up leapt cook-boys, scullions, and all the foul-mouthed rascality of a great medieval household, and attacked Hereward with forks and flesh-hooks.

Then was Hereward aware of a great broach, or spit, before the fire, and recollecting how he had used such a one as a boy against the monks of Peterborough, was minded to use it again against the cooks of Brandon; which he did so heartily, that in a few moments he had killed one, and driven the others backward in a heap.

1 In what language were the threats to Hereward spoken?
2 What word is used meaning 'to change into the English language'?
3 Did Hereward really understand French?
4 What did Hereward do when one man pulled his beard?
5 What is meant by 'medieval'?

6 With what did the members of the Norman household attack Hereward?
7 How did he defend himself?
8 When before had he used this means of defence?
9 Where was this 'medieval household'?
10 Do you know what Hereward is sometimes called? Where was his stronghold?

19

(A) *Moby Dick*, **one of the first really great books written in America, was published in 1851. It was written by Herman Melville, an American of Scottish extraction; born in New York in 1815, died 1891. Read this extract from the book and then answer the questions.**

Call me Ishmael. Some years ago—never mind how long precisely—having little or no money in my purse, and nothing particular to interest me on shore, I thought I would sail about a little and see the watery part of the world. It is a way I have of driving off the spleen, and regulating the circulation. Whenever I find myself growing grim about the mouth: whenever it is a damp, drizzly November in my soul; whenever I find myself involuntarily pausing before coffin warehouses, and bringing up the rear of every funeral I meet—then, I account it high time to get to sea as soon as I can.

Now, when I say that I am in the habit of going to sea, whenever I begin to grow hazy about the eyes, and begin to be over conscious of my lungs, I do not mean to have it inferred that I ever go to sea as a passenger. For to go as a passenger you must needs have a purse, and a purse is but a rag unless you have something in it. Besides, passengers get sea-sick— grow quarrelsome—don't sleep of nights—do not enjoy themselves much, as a general thing; no, I never go as a passenger; nor, though I am something of a salt, do I ever go to sea as a Commodore, or a Captain, or a Cook. I abandon the glory and distinction of such offices to those who like them.

1 Why did Ishmael first decide to go to sea?
2 How did he think it would restore him to health?

3 What do you need to go to sea as a passenger?
4 What four things often happen to passengers at sea?
5 In what capacity do you imagine Ishmael went to sea?
6 Two naval officers are mentioned. Who are they?
7 Name any three VERBS in the extract.
8 Two NOUNS suggest something rather gloomy. What are they?
9 What would you say is the meaning of a 'salt'?
10 What kind of weather does the writer evidently think is typical of November?
11 In what connection does he use this phrase?

(B) **Read the following extract from** *The Essays of Elia* **by Charles Lamb (1775-1834). It is called**

THE DISCOVERY OF ROAST PORK

The swine-herd, Ho-ti, having gone out into the woods one morning, as his manner was, to collect mast for his hogs, left his cottage in the care of his eldest son Bo-bo, a great lubberly boy, who, being fond of playing with fire, as younkers of his age commonly are, let some sparks escape into a bundle of straw, which kindling quickly, spread the conflagration over every part of their poor mansion till it was reduced to ashes. Together with the cottage (a sorry antediluvian make-shift of a building, you may think it), what was of much more importance, a fine litter of new-farrowed pigs, no less than nine in number, perished. China pigs have been esteemed a luxury all over the East from the remotest periods that we read of. Bo-bo was in the utmost consternation, as you may think, not so much for the sake of the tenement, which his father and he could easily build up again with a few dry branches, and the labour of an hour or two, at any time, as for the loss of the pigs.

Answer the following questions:—

1 What was Ho-ti?
2 What did he do every morning?

3 What kind of youth was his eldest son Bo-bo?
4 What was Bo-bo fond of doing?
5 What is meant by
   (a) antediluvian?
   (b) kindling?
   (c) tenement?
6 What perished in the fire?
7 What worried Bo-bo more than anything else?
8 What part of speech is each of the following:—
   (a) Ho-ti? (b) spread? (c) easily? (d) remotest?

(C) **Read this extract on HUNTING TURTLES' EGGS, from** *Tom Sawyer*, **by Mark Twain.**

> After dinner, all the gang turned out to hunt for turtle eggs on the bar. They went about poking sticks into the sand, and when they found a soft place they went down on their knees and dug with their hands. Sometimes they would take fifty or sixty eggs out of one hole. They were perfectly round, white things, a trifle smaller than an English walnut. They had a famous fried-egg feast that night, and another on Friday morning. After breakfast they went whooping and prancing out on the bar, and chased each other round and round, shedding clothes as they went, until they were naked, and then continued the frolic far away up the shoal water of the bar, against the stiff current, which latter tripped their legs from under them from time to time, and greatly increased the fun. And now and then they stood in a group and splashed water in each other's faces with their palms, gradually approaching each other with averted faces, to avoid the straggling sprays, and finally gripping and struggling till the best man ducked his neighbour, and then they all went under in a tangle of white legs and arms, and came up blowing, sputtering, laughing, and gasping for breath at one and the same time.

Now answer these questions.

1 What do you think is meant by "on the bar"?

2 How many turtle eggs would they sometimes find in one hole?
3 Briefly describe a turtle's egg.
4 What effect did the stiff current have upon the gang?
5 What is the meaning of "averted faces"?
6 Describe briefly how they came up after the ducking.
7 Give a *different meaning* to the following words which are found in the extract:—
   (a) trifle (b) palms (c) sprays.
8 What phrases refer to *a definite time*?

20

(A) **Read the following. It is from an historical novel called** *Harold*, **by Lord Lytton (1803-1873). It is about the death of King Harold at the Battle of Hastings.**

"Look up, look up, and guard thy head," cries the fatal voice of Haco to the King.

At that cry the King raises his flashing eyes. Why halts his stride? Why drops the axe from his hand? As he raised his head, down came the hissing death shaft. It smote the lifted face; it crushed into the dauntless eyeball. He reeled, he staggered, he fell back several yards, at the foot of the gorgeous standard. With desperate hand he broke the head of the shaft, and left the barb, quivering in the anguish.

Gurth knelt over him.

"Fight on," gasped the King, "conceal my death. Holy Crosse! England to the rescue. Woe—woe."

Rallying himself a moment, he sprang to his feet, clenched his right hand, and fell once more—a corpse.

At the same moment a simultaneous rush of horsemen towards the standard bore back a line of Saxons, and covered the body of the King with heaps of the slain.

Answer the following:—

1 Why did Haco tell the King to look up and guard his head?

2   What happened to the King?
3   What did he wish the army to do?
4   What word is given which means 'a rush of horsemen together'?
5   Whom do you think was Haco?
6   What is meant by 'the hissing death shaft'?
7   What would be the 'gorgeous standard'?
8   What word in the passage means 'a dead body'?

(B)   **Read this description of a medieval castle, from an historical novel, *Quentin Durward*, by Sir Walter Scott (1771-1832).**

There were three external walls, battlemented and turreted from space to space, and at each angle, the second enclosure rising higher than the first, and being built so as to command the exterior defence in case it was won by the enemy; and being again, in the same manner, itself commanded by the third and innermost barrier. Around the external wall, as the Frenchman informed his young companion (for, as they stood lower than the foundation of the wall, he could not see it), was sunk a ditch of about twenty feet in depth, supplied with water by a dam-head on the river Cher, or rather on one of its tributary branches. In front of the second enclosure, he said, there ran another fosse, and a third, both of the same unusual dimensions, was led between the second and the innermost enclosure. The verge, both of the outer and inner circuit of this triple moat, was strongly fenced with palisades of iron, serving the purpose of what are called "chevaux-de-frise" in modern fortification, the top of each pale being divided into a cluster of sharp spikes, which seemed to render any attempt to climb over an act of self-destruction.

From within the innermost enclosure arose the Castle itself, containing buildings of different periods, crowded around, and united with the ancient and grim-looking donjon-keep, which was older than any of them, and which rose, like a black Ethiopian giant, high into the air, while the absence of any windows larger than shot-holes, irregularly disposed for defence, gave the spectator the same unpleasant feeling which we experience on looking at a blind man.

Answer the following:—

1 Give two words which mean 'outside'.
2 About how deep was the ditch?
3 What was the name of the river which supplied it with water?
4 Give another name for a ditch or moat.
5 What is meant by 'chevaux-de-frise'?
6 What really amounted to an act of self-destruction?
7 What word is sometimes used instead of 'self-destruction'?
8 Which was the oldest part of the castle?
9 What did it resemble?
10 What sort of windows did the keep have?

(C) **Read this extract about "How Aladdin entered the cave", from** *Tales from the Arabian Nights,* **and then attempt the questions that follow.**

Aladdin jumped into the opening, and went down the steps. He found the three chambers and passed through them to the garden. Then, without stopping, he ascended to the terrace. He took the lamp which stood lighted in the niche, threw out its contents, and put it in his bosom. On his way back through the garden he stopped to look more carefully at the fruit, which he had only glanced at before. The fruit of each tree had a separate colour. Some were white, others sparkling and transparent; some were red; others green, blue, or violet; some of a yellowish hue, in short, there were fruits of almost every colour. The white were pearls; the sparkling and transparent fruits were diamonds; the deep red were rubies; the green emeralds; the blue turquoises; the violet amethysts; those tinged with yellow sapphires. All were of the largest size, and the most perfect ever seen in the world, but Aladdin thought they were only pieces of coloured glass. Yet the variety and contrast of so many beautiful colours, as well as the brilliancy and great size of these fruits, tempted him to gather some of each kind; and he took so many of every colour, that he filled all his pockets, and stuffed others in his girdle and inside his shirt, until he had no room for more.

1. What did Aladdin have to pass through in order to reach the garden?
2. What is meant by a 'terrace'?
3. Where did he find the lamp?
4. What attracted Aladdin's attention in the garden?
5. What was remarkable about the fruit of each tree?
6. Which words best described diamonds?
7. Which precious stones are coloured
   (a) green (b) red (c) blue (d) violet?
8. What did Aladdin think the jewels were?
9. What tempted him to gather some of each kind?
10. Where did he put them when he had gathered them?

21

(A) *South With Scott*, by E. R. G. R. Evans.
The following extract, which is taken from this book, deals with the explorers' first sight of Antarctica. Read it carefully and then attempt the questions that follow.

We sighted our first iceberg in latitude 62° on the evening of Wednesday, December 7. Cheetham's squeaky hail came down from aloft and I went up to the crow's-nest to look at it, and from this time on we passed all kinds of icebergs, from the huge tubular variety to the little weathered water-worn bergs. Some we steamed quite close to and they seemed for all the world like great masses of sugar floating in the sea.

From latitude 60° to 63° we saw a fair number of birds; southern fulmars, whale birds, molly-mawks, sooty albatrosses, and occasionally Cape-pigeons still. Then the brown-backed petrels began to appear, sure precursors of the pack ice—it was in sight right enough the day after the brown-backs were seen. By breakfast time on December 9, when nearly in latitude 65°, we were steaming through thin streams of broken pack with floes from six to twelve feet across. A few penguins and seals were seen, and by 10 a.m. no less than twenty-seven icebergs were in sight. The newcomers to these regions were clustered in little groups on the forecastle and poop, sketching and painting, hanging over the bows and gleefully watching this lighter stuff being brushed aside by our strong stem.

1 Which member of the crew first saw the iceberg?
2 Where was he?
3 In what latitude was the first iceberg sighted?
4 What did the icebergs look like?
5 Which bird is reputed to be a bird of ill omen?
6 Which birds were "sure precursors of the pack ice"?
7 How many icebergs were seen on December 9th?
8 What did the newcomers do?
9 What do you think is meant by the 'strong stem'?
10 What two special varieties of icebergs are mentioned?

(B) **Read this extract from** *The Ascent of Everest,* **by Sir John Hunt; it deals with their final preparations.**

Pressmen and other onlookers had come to see us off and there was much clicking of cameras as the long stream of coolies started off into the town on their way eastwards. Some of them carried loads which, although they conformed to the standard weight of 60lb., had a forbidding appearance. One of these was our metal ladder, each length of which measured six feet. An even more formidable monster was a shining aluminium trunk of coffin-like dimensions, in which Griffith Pugh's modest needs were housed. This object was treated with respect by the coolies and caused the rest of us some merriment. It is greatly to Griff's credit that he insisted, despite protests and jests on all sides, on having it transported all the way to our Base Camp at the foot of the Icefall.

Later that morning, I returned to the Embassy with Colonel Proud, the First Secretary, and three members of the party who were to travel with the second caravan. I heaved yet another of many sighs of relief; at last we were on the final stage of our approach to the mountain—planning and preparation had given place to action.

Now answer the following:—

1   Who came to see the party off?
2   What do you understand by the 'clicking of cameras'?
3   What was the standard weight carried by a coolie?
4   What two items of equipment are especially mentioned?
5   What is meant by the 'Embassy'?
6   Why was Sir John Hunt relieved?
7   What metal is mentioned here?
8   What is its special quality?
9   Give a word from the extract which means
    (a) something to be dreaded (b) measurements (c) carried.
10 (a) Find from your atlas the range of mountains in which Everest is situated.
    (b) Give the height of Everest.

(C) **Miss Pat Smythe is a famous horsewoman as many of you may know. The following extract is taken from her book,** *Jump for Joy.*

The Channel was rough and the Captain hummed and hawed about whether he would allow us to sail; he obviously regretted his decision when we hit the storm soon after leaving harbour. The crossing was terrible, with sea water pouring across the decks and into the sheltered holds where Leona, the pony, and the mares were standing. The horses were soon soaked and at one stage we grew nervous for their safety, for the rolling ship tossed about the valuable mares, some of them heavy in foal, they slithered pitifully around the wet plank flooring and there was little we could do to soothe them. Eventually we reached Boulogne, where I put my two horses into the goods train that would take us non-stop across France. The goods van was old, and could have been scrawled with the words of that classic inscription from the First World War: 40 Men, or 8 Horses. Before the train pulled out I had fifteen minutes to make a dash for the nearest "épicerie" where I bought a bottle of red wine and a large cheese; it was now dark, and I could not find a place to buy bread.

Answer these questions:—

1 What is meant here by the 'Channel'?
2 What does the phrase mean, 'hummed and hawed'?
3 What kind of weather was it when they left harbour?
4 In what part of the ship were the horses?
5 What harm did the horses suffer from the storm?
6 Give another word for 'slithered'.
7 What does it mean by the train 'pulled out'?
8 What kind of shop do you think an "épicerie" is?
9 Where did the ship land in France?
10 What was it that the writer was unable to buy?

Can you say *when* was the First World War?

22

(A) Read the following passage carefully and then answer the questions about it.

Peat, although it is of the same origin as coal and has the same chemical constituents, is not a true coal. It is found in thick bogs or swamps, of which the best known are in Ireland, although there are also large deposits in Scotland and England. In the natural state it may contain more than nine-tenths water, and even after being cut and dried the amount of moisture in it may still be as much as a quarter. The amount of water in peat and its low heating value are considerable disadvantages. It is usually burnt in open fires. It needs a good draught to light it, but it will burn slowly, and if a large piece is put on top of a coal fire it will help to keep it in. Considerable labour is needed to cut and stack peat, and it cannot be easily transported, thus limiting its economic use to the localities where it is found.

1 What are the main two disadvantages of peat?
2 In what sort of places is peat usually found?
3 Why is peat only used in the area where it is found?
4 Give two advantages mentioned in the use of peat.
5 What does peat mainly consist of in its natural state?
6 Look at the following example:—
   length (noun), long (adjective), lengthen (verb).
   With this example to guide you, write out the following on your paper and fill in the blanks:—

NOUN	ADJECTIVE	VERB
Moisture	....	....
Origin	....	....

(B) Now read this passage and then answer the questions about it.

Everyone knows, of course, that Brazil is the world's greatest coffee-growing country, but it is hard to realise that it produces nearly 75% of the world's coffee. Coffee grows in many different parts of Brazil, but more than half the country's crop is produced in this region round about Sao Paulo. That can perhaps make us understand how concentrated coffee production is in this very small area. Does it not seem strange that this section should be so spectacularly superior to all others in the world for the growing of coffee? Let us see why this is true. The main reason is the soil, a reddish soil which seems to contain exactly the elements that coffee requires. Then, too, the land is high, being spread out on the surface of that plateau whose slope we ascended just outside Santos, and high altitude, as we know already, is favourable to coffee. The climate is such that sunshine can be counted on when the coffee needs it for the drying process. And the nearness to the coast makes export convenient and inexpensive.

1 Name four reasons why the region round Sao Paulo is favourable to growing coffee.
2 Give words opposite in meaning to
   (a) ascend (b) convenient (c) superior (d) drying (e) export.
3 Say if the following statements are TRUE or UNTRUE:
   (a) Nearly 75% of the world's coffee is produced in the region around Sao Paulo.
   (b) Coffee needs sunshine for the drying process.
   (c) All reddish soils are suitable for growing coffee.
4 In what country is Sao Paulo situated?
5 In what continent is this country?

(C) **Read this extract from a modern bicycle catalogue and then attempt the questions that follow.**

RALEIGH PATENT AUTOMATIC FILTER SWITCH UNIT

Standard equipment on all 'Superbes', incorporating the following striking advantages: With the headlamp switch in the 'on' position, light is given at all times, whether the machine is stationary or in motion. Whilst stationary and at very low speeds, three standard dry battery LEAK-PROOF cells provide the light. As speed increases the Filter Switch automatically cuts out the batteries and changes over to the 'Dynohub'. This procedure is reversed as speed decreases.

The Filter Switch is foolproof, having no moving parts and requiring no service.

Keeps usage of battery current to a minimum at slow speed and this ensures long battery life.

When batteries are exhausted they should be removed. The set will operate as a direct lighting unit until new ones are fitted.

A REVELATION IN CYCLE LIGHTING—UNIQUE, SIMPLE, TROUBLE-FREE.

1 What is standard equipment on all "Raleigh Superbe" bicycles?
2 When can you get light at all times?
3 What is meant by the machine being 'stationary' ?
4 There is another word pronounced the same as 'stationary' but it has a totally different meaning. Give this word and say what it means.
5 When the machine is stationary and when travelling at low speeds, how is light provided?
6 When speed increases how is light then provided?
7 Why is the filter-switch foolproof?
8 What would you say is meant by 'foolproof'?
9 What is another advantage of the filter-switch?
10 (a) What is another meaning of the word "current"?
   (b) A word is pronounced like 'current' but has a different meaning. Give this word and say what it means.
   (c) What is the opposite word to "minimum"?

23

(A) Read this extract from the *Diary of Samuel Pepys* (1633-1703) **for September 2nd, 1666, in which he gives a vivid account of the Great Fire of London, 1666.**

So down, with my heart full of trouble, to the Lieutenant of the Tower, who tells me that it begun this morning in the King's baker's house in Pudding-lane, and that it hath burned down St. Magnus's Church and most part of Fish Street already. So I down to the water-side, and there got a boat, and through bridge, and there saw a lamentable fire. Poor Michell's house, as far as the Old Swan, already burned that way, and the fire running further, that, in a very little time, it got as far as the Steele-yard, while I was there. Every body endeavouring to remove their goods, and flinging into the river, or bringing them into lighters that lay off; poor people staying in their houses as long as till the very fire touched them, and then running into boats, or clambering from one pair of stairs, by the waterside, to another. And, among other things, the poor pigeons, I perceive, were loth to leave their houses, but hovered about the windows and balconys, till they burned their wings, and fell down. Having staid, and in an hour's time seen the fire rage every way; and nobody, to my sight, endeavouring to quench it, but to remove their goods, and leave all to the fire; and, having seen it get as far as the Steele-yard, and the wind mighty high, and driving it into the City; and everything after so long a drought, proving combustible, even the very stones of churches; and, among other things, the poor steeple by which pretty Mrs —— lives, and whereof my old schoolfellow Elborough is parson, taken fire in the very top, and there burned till it fell down; I to White Hall, with a gentleman with me, who desired to go off from the Tower, to see the fire, in my boat; and there up to the King's closet in the Chapel, where people come about me, and I did give them an account dismayed them all, and word was carried in to the King. So I was called for, and did tell the King and the Duke of York what I saw; and that, unless his Majesty did command houses to be pulled down, nothing could stop the fire.

Now answer the following:—

1. Where did the Great Fire of London start?
2. After he had visited the Lieutenant of the Tower, where did Pepys go?
3. How were most people trying to save their goods?
4. What happened to the pigeons?
5. What helped the fire to burn so fiercely?
6. What kind of weather had there been sometime before the Fire?
7. How did Pepys suggest that the fire could be checked?
8. Where apparently did the King reside?
9. Who was Pepys's old schoolfellow and what did he do for a living?
10. Do you know what terrible calamity preceded the Great Fire?

(B) William Cobbett, the son of a farmer, born at Farnham in 1762, made an interesting journey throughout southern England on horseback, staying at farms and enquired from farmers, labourers, and anyone who would talk to him, about anything that concerned farming matters. In his *Rural Rides*, this is what he wrote on December 4th, 1821, from Elverton Farm, near Faversham, Kent.

> This is the first time, since I went to France, in 1792, that I have been on this side of Shooters' Hill. The land, generally speaking, from Deptford to Dartford is poor, and the surface ugly by nature, to which ugliness there has been made, just before we came to the latter place, a considerable addition by the inclosure of a common, and by the sticking up of some shabby-genteel houses, surrounded with dead fences and things called gardens, in all manner of ridiculous forms, making, all together the bricks, hurdle-rods, and earth say as plainly as they can speak, "Here dwell *vanity* and poverty". This is a little excrescence that has grown out of the immense sums, which have been drawn from other parts of the kingdom to be expended on barracks, magazines, martello-towers, catamarans, and all the excuses for lavish expenditure, which the war for the Bourbons gave rise to. All things will return; these rubbishy flimsy things on this common, will first be deserted, then crumble down, then be swept away, and the cattle, sheep, pigs and geese will once more graze upon the common, which will again furnish heath, furze and turf for the labourers on the neighbouring lands.

Now try and answer the following questions:—

1 What foreign country had Cobbett visited?
2 Where did he think the land was especially poor?
3 What do you think is meant by the "inclosure of a common"?
4 What does Cobbett say was erected in this 'inclosure'?
5 What does he seem to think of gardens?
6 What words from the passage suggest military buildings?
7 What would once more graze on the common after it had been restored?

8 With what would the common once more supply the neighbours?

9 What parts of speech are the following words:—
   (a) ridiculous, (b) inclosure, (c) surrounded, (d) away, (e) which?

(C) John Wesley (1703-91), like Cobbett, was a great traveller. It has been estimated that he travelled 250,000 miles, mostly on horseback, in all parts of the British Isles. He often received very rough treatment as is shown from this extract from his *Journals*, dated August 28th, 1748.

> At one I went to the Cross in Bolton. There was a vast number of people, but many of them utterly wild. As soon as I began speaking, they began thrusting to and fro; endeavouring to throw me down from the steps on which I stood. They did so once or twice; but I went up again and continued my discourse. They then began to throw stones; at the same time some got upon the cross behind me to push me down; on which I could not but observe, how God overrules even the minutest circumstances. One man was bawling, just at my ear, when a stone struck him on the cheek, and he was still.
>
> A second was forcing his way down to me, till another stone hit him on the forehead, it bounded back, the blood ran down, and he came no farther. The third, being got close to me, stretched out his hand, and in the instant a sharp stone came upon the joints of his fingers. He shook his hand, and was very quiet till I concluded my discourse and went away.

Answer the following:—

1 What do you think is meant by 'the Cross'?

2 In what county is Bolton situated?

3 How would you describe the behaviour of many of the people?

4 What did they try to do to Wesley?

5 What is meant by 'discourse'?

6 What happened to the first man who was shouting at Wesley?

7 What happened to the second man?

8 Where was the third man hit?

9 To whom did Wesley attribute his escape?

10 Do you know what the followers of Wesley are today called?

24

(A) **Read this extract from** *The Farmer as Nature Lover*, **by Doreen Wallace.**

The farmer is Nature's husband, not her lover. Ecstasies at her beauty are not his. He has lived with beauty all his life; and familiarity has bred, not perhaps contempt, but a quite unemotional acceptance of Nature's most striking efforts at adornment. A flaming sunset moves him to think of the morrow, a lowering flushed dawn makes him hastily rearrange in his head the work he had planned for the day. Spring in her lacy green, frilled with white fool's-parsley, irritates him, as often as not, because she will not weep, or else she weeps too much. With Summer he quarrels constantly; her splendour of blue-black cloud in sunshine, against which the heavy-clad trees gleam out as though cut in metal, means thunder to spoil the haysel, thunder to lay flat the tall, unripe corn, or thunder to delay harvest. With Autumn he is usually on better terms, for a really wet autumn, which would hold up the ploughing and make the harvesting of sugar-beet laborious and expensive, is happily uncommon. But perhaps it is in winter that he is most nearly at peace with Nature. There is a brief lull in his eternal battle against Time. There is the ploughing after root-crops to be done, for the reception of the spring sowings, but there is time in addition for the tidying-up so dear to the good farmer's heart—the "flashing" of ditches, the trimming and laying of fences, the mending of gates. Smoke of bonfires dims the day, between the mists of the morning and evening frost.

Now see if you can answer these questions:—

1 What well-known proverb is more or less formulated in the first few lines of this extract?

2 Why does the farmer re-arrange his work for the day when he sees a 'flushed dawn'?

3   Why is the farmer sometimes irritated by the Spring?
4   Why does he constantly quarrel with Summer?
5   Why is he usually on better terms with Autumn?
6   Give at least *three* operations which can be carried out by the farmer during the winter months.
7   Why is it that during Winter the farmer is 'most nearly at peace with Nature'?
8   What havoc can a thunderstorm cause in summer?

(B)   **Read the following extract about ANTS and then answer the questions that follow.**

Like bees and wasps, some kinds of ants are equipped with stings. Others lack these weapons, and their poison sac serves as a reservoir whence venom, usually formic acid which has a toxic and corrosive action, is squirted from an aperture at the tip of the abdomen. Some stingless ants first bite their enemy with their jaws, then spray poison into the wound, a rather cumbersome method involving two separate and distinct operations. But stingless ants also use their poison collectively to set up a kind of tear-gas barrage. When a nest is attacked, and its outer defences partly demolished by the enemy, the sterile females, or workers, hurry to points of vantage and eject their formic acid into the air. The pungent fumes tend to disconcert and drive away the foe; and there can be little doubt that ant battles are frequently decided without a single wound being inflicted by either army.

1   How do some kinds of ants resemble bees and wasps?
2   What is the chemical name of the substance ejected from the abdomen of the stingless ants?
3   With what two operations do the stingless ants attack their prey?
4   What do the workers do when the nest is attacked?
5   How is it that ant battles are often decided without a single wound being inflicted?

6 Can you give other words from the passage which mean
(a) poison (b) an opening (c) clumsy (d) upset or disturb (e) to throw out or emit?
7 What is meant here by a 'tear-gas barrage'?
8 What word in the passage can also be used to describe a place where a large amount of water is stored?

(C) **Read this extract about** *The Earliest Motor Cars,* **and then attempt the questions.**

It was in Germany and France that the first successful attempts were made to produce an internal-combustion engine driven by petrol. In England people were strangely timid about horseless vehicles. English inventors were handicapped by a quaint old law which forbade any such vehicle to attain a greater speed than four miles an hour, and compelled each one to be preceded by a man carrying a red flag. This law was not repealed until 1896.

The earliest motor cars were looked upon as mere jokes, or as rather dangerous playthings, by every one except their inventors. Some of them were single-seaters, others could carry two, or even three, people; but all were noisy, clumsy, queer-looking things. When in 1888, Carl Benz, a German, produced a three-wheeled, internal-combustion car, a great forward stride had been made. Another German, whose name, Daimler, is often seen on motor cars to this day, was experimenting about the same time, and testing a petrol-driven engine.

It is easy to understand how the introduction of the petrol-driven engine revolutionized road transport throughout the world. Until then the necessary power to push a vehicle along could not be obtained without the cumbersome tanks and boilers and furnaces of the steam engine. The internal-combustion engine is light in weight and small in size by comparison; the fuel is burned *in* it, so that there is no waste, like the dusty cinders of a coal-fire.

1 In what countries were the first successful attempts made to produce an internal combustion engine?

2   How were English inventors handicapped?
3   How did most people regard early motor cars?
4   What were all early motor cars?
5   When was a great step forward made regarding early motor cars?
6   Who was often seen experimenting in early motor cars about the same time as Benz?
7   What was the speed of these early cars?
8   Mention any four modern makes of motor cars.
9   Mention any three advantages of the internal combustion engine.
10 What does "repealed" mean?

25

(A) **Read this extract from the popular story *The Prisoner of Zenda*, by Anthony Hope, and then answer the questions.**

As soon as we reached the Ruritanian frontier (where the old officer who presided over the Custom House favoured me with such a stare that I felt surer than before of my Elphberg physiognomy), I bought the papers, and found in them news which affected my movements. For some reason, which was not clearly explained, and seemed to be something of a mystery, the date of the coronation had been suddenly advanced, and the ceremony was to take place on the next day but one. The whole country seemed in a stir about it, and it was evident that Strelsau was thronged. Rooms were all let and hotels overflowing; there would be very little chance of my obtaining a lodging, and I should certainly have to pay an exorbitant charge for it. I made up my mind to stop at Zenda, a small town fifty miles short of the capital, and about ten from the frontier. My train reached there in the evening; I would spend the next day, Tuesday, in a wander over the hills, which were said to be very fine, and in taking a glance at the famous Castle, and go over by train to Strelsau on the Wednesday morning, returning at night to sleep at Zenda.

1   When they reached the Ruritanian frontier, what building did they enter?

2 For what purpose do you think they entered this place?
3 What news did the writer find in the papers?
4 What was happening at Strelsau?
5 What does 'exorbitant' mean?
6 Where did the writer make up his mind to stay?
7 What day did he reach there?
8 How did he resolve to spend Tuesday?
9 What do you think the writer means by his "Elphberg *physiognomy*"?

(B) **The romantic story of the conquest of Mexico by the Spaniards under Cortés (1518 to 1521) is told by Prescott in his** *History of the Conquest of Mexico*, **from which the following passage is taken. Read it carefully and then answer the questions that follow.**

> On his return to the camp, Cortés found a new cause of disquietude, in discontents which had broken out among the soldiery. Their patience was exhausted by a life of fatigue and peril to which there seemed no end. Among the malcontents were a number of noisy, vapouring persons, such as are found in every camp, who, like empty bubbles, are sure to rise to the surface and make themselves seen in seasons of agitation. They now waited on the general, not in a mutinous spirit of resistance, but with the design of frank expostulation, as with a brother adventurer in a common cause. Their sufferings, they told him, were too great to be endured. All the men had received one, most of them two or three wounds. More than fifty had perished in one way or another. There was no beast of burden but led a life preferable to theirs. For, when the night came, the former could rest from his labours; but they, fighting or watching, had no rest, day nor night. Cortés listened to this singular expostulation with perfect composure. He knew his men, and, instead of rebuke or harsher measures, replied in the same frank and soldier-like vein which they had effected.

1 Why was there discontent in Cortés' army?
2 Who took the lead among the malcontents?

3 To what are they compared?
4 Complete the proverb, "Empty vessels ------------------."
5 What did the men tell him about their sufferings?
6 How many had died in one way or another?
7 Whom did they say led a life preferable to theirs?
8 How did Cortés listen to the complaints of his men?
9 Cortés was a great Spanish general. Name any other three great generals in history.
10 Mention another word pronounced like "vein" but with a totally different meaning. Give its meaning.

(C) **Read the following extract on A DOUR YORKSHIREMAN, MR. YORKE, from the novel *Shirley*, by Charlotte Brontë (1816-1855).**

A Yorkshire gentleman he was, *par excellence*, in every point; about fifty-five years old, but looking at first sight still older, for his hair was silver white. His forehead was broad, not high; his face fresh and hale; the harshness of the north was seen in his features, as it was heard in his voice; every trait was thoroughly English—not a Norman line anywhere; it was an inelegant, unclassic, unaristocratic mould of visage. Fine people would perhaps have called it vulgar; sensible people would have termed it characteristic; shrewd people would have delighted in it for the pith, sagacity, intelligence, the rude yet real originality marked in every lineament, latent in every furrow. But it was an indocile, a scornful, and a sarcastic face—the face of a man difficult to lead, and impossible to drive. His stature was rather tall, and he was well-made and wiry, and had a stately integrity of port; there was not a suspicion of the clown about him anywhere.

Answer the following:—

1 How old was the Yorkshire gentleman?
2 Why did he appear older?
3 What made it appear that he came from the North?

4 Describe his face.
5 How would fine people have described it?
6 Why would shrewd people have delighted in it?
7 What makes you think he was a stubborn character?
8 Describe his build.
9 What sentence leads you to suppose he was a serious type of man?
10 Two words are used here in connection with facial features, namely "mould" and "furrow".
   (a) Give another meaning of "mould".
   (b) Also give another meaning of "furrow".
11 What is meant by these words?
   (a) Sagacity (b) integrity (c) lineament.

26

(A) **William Makepeace Thackeray (1811-1863) wrote a great novel called** *Vanity Fair,* **from which this extract is taken. It is about THE BATTLE OF WATERLOO, 1815.**

All our friends took their share and fought like men in the great field. All day long, whilst the women were praying ten miles away, the lines of the dauntless English infantry were receiving and repelling the furious charges of the French horsemen. Guns which were heard at Brussels were ploughing up their ranks, and comrades falling, and the resolute survivors closing in. Towards evening, the attack of the French repeated and resisted so bravely, slackened in its fury. They had other foes besides the British to engage, or were preparing for a final onset. It came at last: the columns of the Imperial Guard marched up the hill of Saint Jean, at length and at once to sweep the English from the height which they had maintained all day, in spite of all. Unscared by the thunder of the artillery, which hurled death from the English line, the dark rolling column pressed on and on up the hill. It seemed almost to crest the eminence, when it began to wave and falter. Then it stopped, still facing the shot. Then at last the English troops rushed from the post from which no enemy had been able to dislodge them, and the Guard turned and fled.

Now answer these questions:—

1. What did the English women do while the men were fighting the battle?
2. How far away were they from the battlefield?
3. What city is mentioned here and in what country is it situated?
4. What famous English General was victorious at Waterloo?
5. Do you know the name of the French General who opposed him?
6. What famous French regiment was brought against the English as a last resort?
7. By what were they undaunted?
8. Where was the English army situated—on a plain, a valley, or a hill?
9. What words suggest your answer?
10. What were the English infantry doing all day?
11. (a) What adjective describes them?
    (b) What adjective describes the charges of the French horsemen?

(B) Read this extract from a book called *Jane Eyre*, by **Charlotte Bronte (1816-1855)**.

The ground was hard, the air was still, my road was lonely; I walked fast till I got warm, and then I walked slowly to enjoy and analyse the species of pleasure brooding for me in the hour and situation. It was three o'clock; the church bell tolled as I passed under the belfry: the charm of the hour lay in its approaching dimness, in the low-gliding and pale-beaming sun. I was a mile from Thornfield, in a lane noted for wild roses in summer, for nuts and blackberries in autumn, and even now possessing a few coral treasures in hips and haws, but whose best winter delight lay in its utter solitude and leafless repose. If a breath of air stirred, it made no sound here; for there was not a holly, not an evergreen to rustle, and the stripped hawthorn and hazel bushes were as still as the white, worn stones, which causewayed the middle of the path. Far and wide, on each side, there were only fields, where no cattle now browsed; and the little brown birds, which stirred occasionally in the hedge, looked like single russet leaves that had forgotten to drop.

Now answer the following questions:—

1 What time of the year was it, judging from this extract?
2 What time of day was it?
3 What was the lane noted for?
4 What colour do you think is meant by 'coral' and 'russet'?
5 What do you think is meant by 'causewayed'?
6 Why would there be no cattle in the fields?
7 What are compared to 'single russet leaves'?
8 What did the writer find was the greatest charm of the lane?
9 What adjectives describe the following words?
    (a) Ground (b) air (c) road.
10 Would you say the sun was rising or setting?

(C) Francis Bacon was a very famous man who lived from 1561 to 1626. His *Essays* are sometimes rather difficult to understand. Read the following essay OF STUDIES, and see if you can answer the questions.

Read not to contradict and confute, nor to believe and take for granted, nor to find talk and discourse, but to weigh and consider. Some books are to be tasted, others to be swallowed, and some few to be chewed and digested; that is, some books are to be read only in parts; others to be read, but not curiously; and some few to be read wholly, and with diligence and attention. Some books also may be read by deputy, and extracts made of them by others; but that would be only in the less important arguments and the meaner sort of books; else distilled books are like common distilled waters, flashy things. Reading maketh a full man, conference a ready man, and writing an exact man. And

therefore if a man write little, he had need have a good memory;
if he confer little, he had need have a present wit; and if he read
little, he had need have much cunning to seem to know that he
doth not.

'Histories make men wise, poets witty, the mathematics subtile, natural philosophy deep, moral, grave, logic and rhetoric able to contend.'

1. What should be the real object of reading?
2. What does it mean by 'some books are to be tasted'?
3. How should you read those books which are to be 'read wholly'?
4. What can be done with regard to the 'meaner' sort of books?
5. What does the art of writing do to a man's character?
6. If a man does not write much, what must he have?
7. If a man reads very little, what must he pretend?
8. If a man studies logic and rhetoric, what should he be able to do?
9. What is usually meant by
    (a) by deputy (b) distilled waters (c) conference (d) logic?

27

(A) Clarendon, in his *History of the Great Rebellion*, published in 1702-4, gives this account of the CHARACTER OF JOHN HAMPDEN. Read it carefully and see if you can answer the questions that follow.

He was a gentleman of a good family in Buckinghamshire, and born to a fair fortune, and of a most civil and affable deportment. In his entrance into the world, he indulged to himself the licence in sports and exercises and company, which were used by men of the most jolly conversation. Afterwards he retired to a more reserved and melancholy society, yet preserving his own cheerfulness and vivacity, and above all a flowing courtesy to all men. He was rather of reputation in his own country, than of fame in the kingdom, before the business of ship-money: but then he grew the argument of all tongues, every man inquiring who and what he was, that durst, at his own charge, support the liberty and property of the kingdom, and rescue his country, as he thought, from being a prey to the Court. His carriage, throughout this agitation, was with that rare temper and modesty, that they who watched him narrowly to find some advantage against his person, were compelled to give him a just testimony. When this Parliament begun, being returned Knight of the Shire for the county where he lived, the eyes of all men were fixed upon him, as their Country's Father, and the pilot that must steer the vessel through the tempests and rocks which threatened it.

1   In what *county* was Hampden born?
2   What do you think is meant by
    (a) 'Born to a fair fortune'?
    (b) 'Of a most civil and affable deportment'?
3   What pursuits did he follow as a young man?
4   What characteristics did he develop as he grew older?
5   What made him become 'the argument of all tongues'?
6   How did he conduct himself during 'this agitation'?
7   What was his rank when Parliament began?
8   How was he regarded by most men?
9   What was the outlook for the country as depicted here?

(B) **This is an extract from a famous history called** *The Decline and Fall of the Roman Empire,* **by Edward Gibbon (1737-1794). It describes THE COLOSSEUM, in Rome.**

The outside of the edifice was encrusted with marble, and decorated with statues. The slopes of the vast concave, which formed the inside, were filled and surrounded with sixty or eighty rows of seats, of marble likewise, covered with cushions, and capable of receiving with ease above fourscore thousand spectators. Sixty-four vomitories (for by that name the doors were very aptly distinguished) poured the immense multitude; and the entrances, passages, and staircases were contrived with such exquisite skill, that each person arrived at his destined place without trouble or confusion. Nothing was omitted which, in any respect, could be subservient to the convenience and pleasure of the spectators. They were protected from the sun and rain by an ample canopy, occasionally drawn over their heads. The air was continually refreshed by the playing of fountains, and profusely impregnated by the grateful scent of aromatics. In the centre of the edifice, the arena, or stage, was strewed with the finest sand, and successively assumed the most different forms. At one moment it seemed to rise out of the earth like the Garden of the Hesperides, and was afterwards broken into the rocks and caverns of Thrace. The subterraneous pipes conveyed an inexhaustible supply of water; and what had just before appeared a level plain, might be suddenly converted into a wide lake, covered with armed vessels, and replenished with the monsters of the deep.

Now answer the following:—

1 What is meant by 'edifice'?
2 What was there on the outside of the Colosseum and how was it decorated?
3 About how many rows of seats were there?
4 How many people could be accommodated?
5 How many doors were there?
6 Why were they appropriately called 'vomitories'?
7 How were the spectators protected from the weather?
8 How was the air kept fresh?
9 What was there in the centre and what was on the floor?
10 Into what might the arena suddenly become converted?

(C) **In 1874 a man named John Richard Green published** *A Short History of the English People*. **The following extract describes in dignified language the TRIAL AND EXECUTION OF CHARLES I.**

Charles appeared before Bradshaw's Court only to deny its

competence and to refuse to plead, but thirty-two witnesses were examined to satisfy the consciences of his judges, and it was not till the fifth day of the trial that he was condemned to death as a tyrant, traitor, murderer, and enemy of his country. The popular excitement vented itself in cries of "Justice", or "God save your Majesty", as the trial went on, but all save the loud outcries of the soldiers was hushed as Charles passed to receive his doom. The dignity which he had failed to preserve in his long jangling with Bradshaw and the judges returned at the call of death. Whatever had been the faults and follies of his life, "he nothing common did nor mean, upon that memorable scene". Two masked executioners awaited the King as he mounted the scaffold, which had been erected outside one of the windows of the Banqueting House at Whitehall; the streets and roofs were thronged with spectators, and a strong body of soldiers stood drawn up beneath. His head fell at the first blow, and as the executioner lifted it to the sight of all a groan of pity and horror burst from the silent crowd.

Answer the following questions:—

1 Which Court did Charles I appear before?
2 What did Charles refuse to do?
3 How many witnesses were called?
4 Why were they called?
5 On what day of the trial was Charles condemned?
6 How did he meet the news of his death?
7 Where did the execution take place?
8 Do you know on what date this event occurred?
9 Can you give the name of the man who really governed the country after the death of the King?

28

(A) The following extract taken from a modern book on *Woodwork* is about GLUE. Read it carefully and then answer the questions.

The glues chiefly used in woodwork are: animal (generally known as scotch), casein, and resin.

Animal Glue.—A strong and reliable glue if properly prepared and used. It is free from any tendency to stain, but is neither heat nor waterproof. It must be used hot. It can be obtained in cakes or in broken-down crystal form. If the former is used it should be placed in a piece of sacking and broken up small with the hammer. The pieces are placed in a clean container (a glass jar is excellent), covered with water, and left to stand overnight. The container is placed in a saucepan and heated, the glue being stirred until it has mixed freely with the water. It should not be boiled but should be rather above the temperature that can reasonably be borne by the hand. When the brush is lifted from the pot it should run down freely without lumps, yet without breaking up into drops.

To apply glue to a piece of cold wood would cause it to chill. The wood should therefore be heated beforehand, care being taken not to blacken shoulder lines by scorching. Furthermore, the gluing should be done in a warm shop, and everything made ready beforehand, cramps being opened the right amount, cramp shoe blocks prepared, and testing tools ready to hand. Any squeezed-out glue should be wiped off immediately before it sets as it is almost impossible to remove it once it has hardened. When light woods such as sycamore are being glued, a little flake white powder is added to prevent dark glue lines.

1. What are the chief glues used in woodwork?
2. Mention one advantage, and two disadvantages of animal glue.
3. How must it be used?
4. If obtained in 'cake' form, what should first be done with it?
5. After it has been placed in water, how long should it be left to stand?
6. How would you know when the glue was ready for use?
7. Why must the wood be heated before the glue is applied?
8. Where should the gluing be done?
9. Mention the apparatus which must be prepared beforehand.
10. What should be done to any squeezed-out glue?

(B) Read the following passage about LOUIS PASTEUR (1822-1895).

CONQUEROR OF DISEASE

On the field of battle in one of his campaigns, Napoleon decorated for bravery a certain tanner named Pasteur. This brave soldier had an equally brave son, Louis Pasteur, born seven years after Waterloo. He was not a soldier, but he was a fighter. He fought disease. He devoted his life to the study of what we sometimes call germs or microbes which men of science call bacteria, a Greek word meaning "little rods". Bacteria are vegetable organisms which exist in the air, water and soil, and in the bodies of animals and plants; some but not all are the causes of diseases, some convert matter into food for plants.

Louis Pasteur had a very busy and interesting life. He not only made some exciting discoveries about germs but he was able to use his discoveries in very practical ways. He worked hard in his laboratory with test tubes and all kinds of experiments, but nearly all the time he was working to help people who were suffering in some special way from disease. Among the people whom Pasteur was able to help were brewers, breeders of silk worms, and cow keepers, all of whom were trying to carry on important industries in France. Pasteur was always very proud of being able to help his country in this way.

Answer the following:—

1 Give the year in which Louis Pasteur was born.

2 Who was his father?

3 To what did Pasteur devote his life?

4 What would germs or bacteria look like under a microscope?

5 Where are bacteria to be found?

6 What do the 'good' germs do?

7 What industries specially benefited from Pasteur's work?

8 What is a 'tanner'? (Give the occupation, not the slang word sometimes used meaning 'sixpence').

(C) This passage is about ABRAHAM LINCOLN (1809-1865), who has sometimes been described as THE SAVIOUR OF THE U.S.A. Read it and then attempt the questions.

To some Lincoln stands first as the man who freed the slaves of America. Yet he was not a pioneer of this cause. The spadework of the Anti-Slavery movement in America was done by the Abolitionists whom Lincoln disliked and whose policy he opposed. To others Lincoln stands as the saviour of American Union. Yet he only saved it by plunging the country into the horrors of the Civil War—the "Brothers' War"—when many even of his own party urged moderation and compromise upon him. It was a great responsibility, and only a great man could have taken it and earned with it the love and respect of his countrymen.

Abraham Lincoln was born in 1809, the year which also saw the birth of Darwin, Tennyson and Gladstone. He was descended from a Quaker family of English origin who once resided in Pennsylvania. The phrase "From log cabin to White House" has for a long time represented not only the romance of Lincoln's career, but also the chance of any little backwoods-boy to become President of the United States.

1 For what do many people think Abraham Lincoln was first famous?
2 For what do many other people regard him as famous?
3 What other well-known men were born in the same year as Lincoln?
4 Can you say briefly for what each was famous?
5 From what religious sect was Lincoln descended?
6 To what are they firmly opposed?
7 Yet, what did Lincoln plunge his country into?
8 Why did he do this?
9 What is the meaning of 'compromise'?
10 Name any other well-known President of the United States.
11 What is the 'White House'?

29

(A) This is how Edward Gibbon, a famous historian, ended his autobiography. He is the author of *The Decline and Fall of the Roman Empire*. It took him thirty years to write and after he had finished this great work he wrote:—

> It was on the day, or rather night, of the 27th June, 1787, between the hours of eleven and twelve, that I wrote the last lines of the last page, in a summer-house in my garden. After laying down my pen I took several turns in a "berceau", or covered walk of acacias, which commands a prospect of the country, the lake, and the mountains. The air was temperate, the sky was serene, the silver orb of the moon was reflected from the waters, and all nature was silent. I will not dissemble the first emotions of joy on the recovery of my freedom, and perhaps, the establishment of my fame. But my pride was soon humbled, and a sober melancholy was spread over my mind, by the idea that I had taken an everlasting leave of an old and agreeable companion, and that, whatsoever might be the future fate of my "History", the life of the historian must be short and precarious.

Now answer these questions:—

1 Give the exact date when the writer finished his task.
2 Where did he write the last page?
3 What did he do directly after he had completed this work?
4 What were his first feelings immediately after he had finished it?
5 What did he hope he might perhaps achieve?
6 In some respects he felt sorry he had completed his task. What phrase suggests this?
7 What did he conclude about the life of the historian?
8 What are 'acacias'?
9 What is there to indicate that it was a fine night when he had finished his writing?
10 What is the meaning of
   (a) dissemble (b) precarious?

(B) Read this passage from a novel called *The Black Arrow*, by R. L. Stevenson.

THE DEN

The place where Dick had struck the line of a highroad was not far from Holywood, and within nine or ten miles of Shoreby-on-the-Till, and here, after making sure that they were pursued no longer, the two bodies separated. Lord Foxham's followers departed, carrying their wounded master towards the comfort and security of the great abbey; and Dick, as he saw them wind away and disappear in the thick curtain of the falling snow, was left alone with near upon a dozen outlaws, the last remainder of his troop of volunteers.

Some were wounded; one and all were furious at their ill-success and long exposure; and though they were now too cold and hungry to do more, they grumbled and cast sullen looks upon their leaders. Dick emptied his purse among them, leaving himself nothing; thanked them for the courage they had displayed, though he could have found it more readily in his heart to rate them for poltroonery; and having thus somewhat softened the effect of his prolonged misfortune, despatched them to find their way, either severally or in pairs, to Shoreby and the Goat and Bagpipes.

Now answer the following:—

1 What was the nearest place to the point where Dick struck the highroad?
2 Two separate bodies of people are mentioned here. Who are they?
3 Who was wounded and where was he conveyed?
4 What did Dick give to his followers?
5 Although he thanked them for their courage, what would he have rather done?
6 What do you think is probably the name of an inn?
7 The opposites of these words are found in the passage. What are they?
  (a) Appear (b) conscripts (c) shortened (d) cowardice (e) united.

8 (a) Give a noun meaning "poltroonery".
   (b) An adjective meaning "surly".
   (c) A verb meaning "vanish".
   (d) An adverb meaning "one by one".

(C) **This is part of Dr. Johnson's famous letter to the Earl of Chesterfield, dated February 7, 1775. Read it carefully and then see if you can answer the questions that follow.**

> My Lord,
>
> I have lately been informed, by the proprietor of the "World" that two papers, in which my Dictionary is recommended to the public, were written by your Lordship. To be so distinguished is an honour, which, being very little accustomed to favours from the great, I know not well how to receive, or in what terms to acknowledge.
>
> When, upon some slight encouragement, I first visited your lordship, I was overpowered, like the rest of mankind, by the enchantment of your address, and could not forbear to wish that I might boast myself "Le vainqueur du vainqueur de la terre"; (the conqueror of the conqueror of the world), that I might obtain that regard for which I saw the world contending; but I found my attendance so little encouraged, that neither pride nor modesty would suffer me to continue it. When I had once addressed your lordship in public, I had exhausted all the art of pleasing which a retired and uncourtly scholar can possess. I had done all that I could; and no man is well pleased to have his all neglected, be it ever so little.
>
> Seven years, my lord, have now passed, since I waited in your outward rooms, or was repulsed from your door; during which time I have been pushing on my work, through difficulties, of which it is useless to complain, and have brought it, at last, to the verge of publication, without one act of assistance, one word of encouragement, or one smile of favour. Such treatment I did not expect, for I never had a patron before.

1 What do you imagine is meant by "The World"?
2 What was recommended in "The World"?

3   By whom was it recommended?
4   Why did Dr. Johnson first visit the Earl of Chesterfield?
5   How do you think he was first received?
6   When did the Earl of Chesterfield praise the Dictionary?
7   What is meant by a 'patron'?
8   How would you describe the tone of this letter—grateful, thankful, sarcastic?
9   For how long did Dr. Johnson have to wait before his Dictionary was praised by the Earl of Chesterfield?

30

(A)   Read the following passage taken from *The Rise of the Dutch Republic* written in 1856 by an American historian, John Lothrop Motley (1814-1877).

THE RELIEF OF LEYDEN

Meantime, the citizens had grown wild with expectation. A dove had been despatched by Boisot, informing them of his precise position, and a number of citizens accompanied the burgomaster, at nightfall, toward the tower of Hengist. "Yonder", cried the magistrate, stretching out his hand towards Lammen, "yonder, behind that fort, are bread and meat, and brethren in thousands. Shall all this be destroyed by the Spanish guns, or shall we rush to the rescue of our friends?"

"We will tear the fortress to fragments with our teeth and nails", was the reply, "before the relief, so long expected, shall be wrested from us." It was resolved that a sortie, in conjunction with the operations of Boisot, should be made against Lammen with the earliest dawn.

Night descended upon the scene, a pitch-dark night, full of anxiety to the Spaniards, to the armada, to Leyden. Strange sights and sounds occurred at different moments to bewilder the anxious sentinels. A long procession of lights issuing from the fort was seen to flit across the black face of the waters, in the dead of night, and the whole of the city wall, between the Cow-gate and the Tower of Burgundy, fell with a loud crash. The horror-struck citizens thought that the Spaniards were upon them at last; the Spaniards imagined the noise to indicate a desperate sortie of the citizens. Everything was vague and mysterious.

Now answer the following:—

1 In what state of mind were the citizens at the beginning of the siege?
2 By what means did Boisot communicate with the citizens?
3 Give another word for 'burgomaster'.
4 Who were besieging Leyden?
5 What fort is mentioned here?
6 What is meant by 'a sortie'?
7 Name five words from the passage which indicate POSITION.
8 What kind of night was it?
9 What was seen to flit across the water?
10 What section of the city wall fell?
11 What did the citizens think it was?
12 What did the Spaniards imagine it to be?

(B) This is from Macaulay's *Essay on Lord Clive*, dated 1840. Read it carefully and then answer the questions that follow.

Some lineaments of the character of the man were early discerned in the child. There remain letters written by his relations when he was in his seventh year; and from these letters it appears that, even at that early age his strong will and fiery passions, sustained by a constitutional intrepidity which sometimes seemed hardly compatible with soundness of mind, had begun to cause great uneasiness to his family. "Fighting", says one of his uncles, "to which he is out of measure addicted, gives his temper such fierceness and imperiousness, that he flies out on every trifling occasion." The old people of the neighbourhood

95

still remember to have heard from their parents how Bob Clive climbed to the top of the lofty steeple of Market-Drayton, and with what terror the inhabitants saw him seated on a stone spout near the summit. They also relate how he formed all the idle lads of the town into a kind of predatory army, and compelled the shopkeepers to submit to a tribute of half-pence in consideration of which he guaranteed the security of their windows. He was sent from school to school, making very little progress in his learning, and gaining for himself everywhere the character of an exceedingly naughty boy. One of his masters, it is said, was sagacious enough to prophesy that the idle lad would make a great figure in the world. But the general opinion seems to have been that poor Robert was a dunce, if not a reprobate.

1 Which sentence from the passage means "what the boy is, the man is"?

2 To what practice was young Clive especially addicted?

3 What town is mentioned in the passage?

4 In which *county* is this town situated?

5 What did Clive do which caused terror to the inhabitants?

6 What words in this passage mean
  (a) One who is good for nothing?
  (b) Consistent with?
  (c) Wise or showing foresight?
  (d) Preying on or plundering?

7 Why were the shopkeepers compelled to pay a tribute of apples and half-pence?

8 What did one of Clive's masters prophesy?

9 What was the general opinion about him?

10 Give the NOUN corresponding to 'prophesy'. It is pronounced almost the same but spelt differently.

(C) **Read this extract from *Lorna Doone*, published in 1869 by Richard D. Blackmore (1825-1900).**

If anybody cares to read a simple tale told simply, I, John Ridd, of the parish of Oare, in the county of Somerset, yeoman and churchwarden, have seen and had a share in some doings of this neighbourhood, which I will try to set down in order, God sparing my life and memory. And they who light upon this book should bear in mind, not only that I write for the clearing of our parish from ill-fame and calumny, but also a thing which will, I trow, appear too often in it, to wit—that I am nothing more than a plain unlettered man, not read in foreign languages, as a gentleman might be, nor gifted with long words (even in mine own tongue), save what I may have won from the Bible, or Master William Shakespeare, whom, in the face of common opinion, I do value highly. In short, I am an ignoramus, but pretty well for a yeoman.

Now answer the following:—

1. Where was John Ridd born?
2. What office did he hold?
3. For what purpose does he say he wrote this book?
4. What kind of man does he say he was?
5. To what class of society did he belong?
6. What does he say a gentleman ought to be?
7. What author did he value highly?
8. What phrase is used here which is now rather out of date?
9. What is an "ignoramus"?
10. Give another meaning of the word "plain".

31

A) **Read this extract from *Three Men in a Boat*, by Jerome K. Jerome (1859-1927), and then answer the questions.**

They started with breaking a cup. That was the first thing they did. They did that just to show you what they *could* do, and to get you interested.

Then Harris packed the strawberry jam on top of a tomato and squashed it, and they had to pick out the tomato with a teaspoon.

And then it was George's turn, and he trod on the butter. I didn't say anything, but I came over and sat on the edge of the table and watched them. It irritated them more than anything I could have said. I felt that. It made them nervous and excited, and they stepped on things, and put things behind them, and then couldn't find them when they wanted them; and they packed the pies at the bottom, and put heavy things on top, and smashed the pies in.

They upset salt over everything, and as for the butter! I never saw two men do more with one-and-twopence worth of butter in my whole life than they did. After George had got it off his slipper, they tried to put it in the kettle. It wouldn't go in, and what *was* in wouldn't come out. They did scrape it out at last, and put it down on a chair, and Harris sat on it, and it stuck to him, and they went looking for it all over the room.

"I'll take my oath I put it down on that chair", said George, staring at the empty seat.

"I saw you do it myself, not a minute ago", said Harris.

Then they started round the room again looking for it; and then they met again in the centre and stared at one another.

"Most extraordinary thing I ever heard of", said George.

"So mysterious!" said Harris.

Then George got round at the back of Harris and saw it.

"Why, here it is all the time", he exclaimed indignantly.

"Where?" cried Harris, spinning round.

"Stand still, can't you!" roared George, flying after him.

And they got it off, and packed it in the teapot.

1 What was the first thing they did?
2 Where did Harris put the strawberry jam?
3 What did George tread on?
4 What did they pack at the bottom?
5 How much did butter then cost?

6 What was upset over everything?
7 After George had scraped the butter off his slipper, where did they next try to put it?
8 What did they pick out with a teaspoon?
9 Why did Harris say "So mysterious!"?
10 Where in the end did they pack the butter?

(B) Read this passage from *The Children of the New Forest*, by **Captain Frederick Marryat (1792-1848). This is a story of the Civil War between the Cavaliers and Roundheads, 1642-51.**

As we have said before, the orphans were four in number; the two eldest were boys, and the youngest were girls. Edward, the elder boy, was between thirteen and fourteen years old; Humphrey, the second, was twelve; Alice, eleven; and Edith, eight. As it is the history of these young persons which we are about to narrate, we shall say little about them at present, except that for many months they had been under little or no restraint, and less attended to. Their companions were Benjamin, the man who remained in the house, and old Jacob Armitage, who passed all the time he could spare with them. Benjamin was rather weak in intellect, and was a source of amusement rather than otherwise. As for the female servants, one was wholly occupied with her attendance on Miss Judith, who was very exacting, and had a high notion of her own consequence. The other two had more than sufficient employment; as, when there is no money to pay with, everything must be done at home. That, in such circumstances, the boys became boisterous and the little girls became romps, it is not to be wondered at: but their having become so, was the cause of Miss Judith seldom admitting them into her room. It is true that they were sent for once a day, to ascertain if they were in the house, or in existence, but soon dismissed and left to their own resources. Such was the neglect to which these young orphans were exposed. It must, however, be admitted, that this very neglect made them independent and bold, full of health from constant activity, and more fitted for the change which was so soon to take place.

Answer these questions:—

1 How old was the elder boy?
2 How old was the younger girl?
3 What were these brothers and sisters?
4 For several months what had happened to them?
5 Who were their two chief companions?
6 What sort of person was Miss Judith?
7 How many female servants were there?
8 How many people were there altogether?
9 What words in this passage mean
   (a) Rough and noisy?
   (b) Self-reliant?

(C) **Read this extract from *The Talisman*, by Sir Walter Scott. It is about the trial of strength between Richard I and Saladin.**

The glittering broadsword, wielded by both his hands, rose aloft to the King's left shoulder, circled round his head, descended with the sway of some terrific engine, and the bar of iron rolled on the ground in two pieces, as a woodsman would sever a sapling with a hedging-bill.

'By the head of the Prophet, a most wonderful blow!' said the Soldan, critically and accurately examining the iron bar which had been cut asunder; and the blade of the sword was so well tempered as to exhibit not the least token of having suffered by the feat it had performed. He then took the King's hand, and looking on the size and muscular strength which it exhibited, laughed as he placed it beside his own, so lank and thin, so inferior in brawn and sinew.

'Ay, look well', said De Vaux, in English, 'it will be long ere your long jackanape's fingers do such a feat with your fine gilded reaping-hook there.'

'Silence, De Vaux', said Richard; 'by Our Lady, he understands or guesses thy meaning—be not so broad, I pray thee.'

The Soldan, indeed, presently said: 'Something I would fain attempt, though wherefore should the weak show their inferiority in presence of the strong? Yet, each land hath its own exercises, and this may be new to the Melech Ric'. So saying, he took from the floor a cushion of silk and down, and placed it upright on one end. 'Can thy weapon, my brother, sever that cushion?' he said to King Richard.

'No, surely', replied the King; 'no sword on earth, were it the Excalibur of King Arthur, can cut that which opposes no steady resistance to the blow."

'Mark, then', said Saladin; and tucking up the sleeve of his gown, showed his arm, thin indeed and spare, but which constant exercise had hardened into a mass consisting of nought but bone, brawn, and sinew. He unsheathed his scimitar, a curved and narrow blade, which glittered not like the swords of the Franks, but was, on the contrary, of a dull blue colour, marked with ten millions of meandering lines, which showed how anxiously the metal had been welded by the armourer. Wielding this weapon, apparently so inefficient when compared to that of Richard, the Soldan stood resting his weight upon his left foot, which was slightly advanced; he balanced himself a little as if to steady his aim, then stepping at once forward, drew the scimitar across the cushion, applying the edge so dexterously, and with so little apparent effort, that the cushion seemed rather to fall asunder than to be divided by violence.

Now answer these questions:—

1 What did the King do with his broadsword?
2 What is meant by 'to sever a sapling'?
3 Was the sword damaged by the blow?
4 Who was the King's attendant?
5 What is meant by the 'Excalibur' of King Arthur?
6 What did the Soldan do with his scimitar?
7 How is the scimitar described?
8 How would you describe
   (a) The King's hand?
   (b) Saladin's arm?

9   What did Richard lead?

10 Who were the people whom Saladin ruled?

32

(A) **This extract is taken from** *Lark Rise to Candleford*, **A Trilogy by Flora Thompson, with an Introduction by H. J. Massingham. It is about country children going to school about 60 years ago. Read the extract and then answer the questions that follow.**

"School began at nine o'clock, but the hamlet children set out on their mile-and-a-half walk there as soon as possible after their seven o'clock breakfast, partly because they liked plenty of time to play on the road and partly because their mothers wanted them out of the way before house-cleaning began.

Up the long, straight road they straggled, in twos and threes and in gangs, their flat, rush dinner-baskets over their shoulders and their shabby little coats on their arms against rain. In cold weather some of them carried two hot potatoes which had been in the oven, or in the ashes, all night, to warm their hands on the way and to serve as a light lunch on arrival.

They were strong, lusty children, let loose from control, and there was plenty of shouting, quarrelling, and often fighting among them. In more peaceful moments they would squat in the dust of the road and play marbles, or sit on a stone heap and play dibs with pebbles, or climb into the hedges after birds' nests or blackberries, or to pull long trails of bryony to wreathe round their hats. In winter they would slide on the ice on the puddles, or make snowballs—soft ones for their friends, and hard ones with a stone inside for their enemies.

After the first mile or so the dinner-baskets would be raided; or they would creep through the bars of the padlocked field gates for turnips to pare with the teeth and munch, or for handfuls of green pea shucks, or ears of wheat, to rub out the sweet, milky grain between the hands and devour. In spring they ate the young green from the hawthorn hedges, which they called 'bread and cheese', and sorrel leaves from the wayside, which they called 'sour grass', and in autumn there was an abundance of haws and blackberries and sloes and crab-apples for them to feast upon. There was always something to eat, and they ate, not so much because they were hungry as from habit and relish of the wild food."

1. At what time did the hamlet children set out for school?
2. Why did they set out at this early hour?
3. What did they carry over their shoulders?
4. What did some of them carry in cold weather?
5. What two special games did they play?
6. What did they do on the way to school in the winter?
7. What would happen to the dinner baskets after the first mile or so?
8. What did they call "bread and cheese"?
9. What was "sour grass"?
10. What did they eat from the countryside in the autumn?
11. What was their real reason for eating?

(B) **Read this example from Joseph Addison's *Essays*, showing how he begins the autobiography of a shilling.**

Methought the shilling that lay upon the table reared itself upon its edge, and turning the face towards me, opened its mouth, and in a soft silver sound, gave me the following account of his life and adventures:—

"I was born (says he) on the side of a mountain, near a little village of Peru, and made a voyage to England in an ingot, under the convoy of Sir Francis Drake. I was, soon after my arrival, taken out of my Indian habit, refined, naturalized, and put into the British mode, with the face of Queen Elizabeth on one side, and the arms of the country on the other. Being thus equipped, I found in me a wonderful inclination to ramble, and visit all parts of the new world into which I was brought."

(The shilling then falls into the hands of a miser and is put into a chest for several years until the miser's heir breaks open the chest and sends the coin on further rambles.)

Answer these questions:—

1 What do we mean by an "Autobiography"?
2 In what tone was the shilling supposed to have spoken?
3 In what country was the shilling born?
4 What is an 'ingot'?
5 What is meant by "under the convoy of Sir Francis Drake"?
6 What happened to the shilling when it arrived in England?
7 What did the shilling then do?
8 Into whose hands did it fall and by whom was it released?

(C) **Read this speech of Jaques from Shakespeare's** *As You Like It,* **and then answer the questions.**

>All the world's a stage,
>And all the men and women merely players:
>They have their exits and their entrances;
>And one man in his time plays many parts,
>His acts being seven ages. As, first the infant,
>Mewling and puking in the nurse's arms.
>And then the whining schoolboy, with his satchel
>And shining morning face, creeping like snail
>Unwillingly to school. And then the lover,
>Sighing like furnace, with a woeful ballad
>Made to his mistress' eyebrow. Then the soldier,
>Full of strange oaths, and bearded like the pard,
>Jealous in honour, sudden and quick in quarrel,
>Seeking the bubble reputation
>Even in the cannon's mouth. And then the justice,
>In fair round belly with good capon lined,
>With eyes severe and beard of formal cut,
>Full of wise saws and modern instances:
>And so he plays his part. The sixth age shifts
>Into the lean and slipper'd pantaloon,
>With spectacles on nose and pouch on side;
>His youthful hose, well sav'd, a world too wide

For his shrunk shank; and his big manly voice,
Turning again toward childish treble, pipes
And whistles in his sound. Last scene of all,
That ends this strange eventful history,
Is second childishness and mere oblivion,
Sans teeth, sans eyes, sans taste, sans every thing.

1 To what are the world and its inhabitants compared?
2 What is an exit?
3 How is the schoolboy depicted?
4 What does the soldier seek?
5 What is meant by "with good capon lined"?
6 Who is "full of wise saws and modern instances"?
7 What does this mean?
8 Mention any three characteristics of old age.
9 What is meant by the frequent use of the word "sans"?
10 How is a childish voice described?

33

(A) *Alice in Wonderland*, **from which the following extract is taken, was first published in 1865. It was written by the Rev. C. L. Dodgson (1833-98), who called himself "Lewis Carroll". It is a wonderful story of make-believe and many children have read with delight all about the Duchess, the Cheshire Cat, the Dormouse, the Mad Hatter, the White Rabbit, the March Hare, the Mock Turtle, and so forth.**
The Rev. C. L. Dodgson, although he never married, loved children. Curiously enough he was a lecturer in mathematics at Oxford University. Perhaps it was a relief to him to write these humorous stories for children. Read the extract and then answer the questions.

THE MOCK TURTLE'S STORY

The Mock Turtle went on:
   "We had the best of educations—in fact we went to school every day——"

"*I've* been to a day-school too", said Alice; "you needn't be so proud as all that."

"With extras?" asked the Mock Turtle a little anxiously.

"Yes", said Alice, "we learned French and music."

"And washing", said the Mock Turtle.

"Certainly not!" said Alice indignantly.

"Ah! then yours wasn't a really good school", said the Mock Turtle in a tone of great relief. "Now at *ours* they had at the end of the bill 'French, music, *and washing*—extra'."

"You couldn't have wanted it much", said Alice; "living at the bottom of the sea."

"I couldn't afford to learn it", said the Mock Turtle with a sigh. "I only took the regular course."

"What was that?" inquired Alice.

"Reeling and Writhing, of course, to begin with", the Mock Turtle replied; "and then the different branches of Arithmetic—Ambition—Distraction, Uglification, and Derision."

"I never heard of 'Uglification' ", Alice ventured to say. "What is it?"

The Gryphon lifted up both its paws in surprise. "What! Never heard of uglifying!" it exclaimed. "You know what to beautify is, I suppose?"

"Yes", said Alice doubtfully: "it means—to—make—anything—prettier."

"Well, then", the Gryphon went on, "If you don't know what to uglify is, you *must* be a simpleton."

1 What was the actual name of the author of *Alice in Wonderland?*

2 What did he call himself?

3 When an author writes under an assumed name, how is this sometimes described?

4 What was the Rev. C. L. Dodgson's occupation?

5 What were the "extras" that Alice learned at school?

6 Why did the Mock Turtle say that it was not a good school?

7 What is meant by "Reeling and Writhing"?

What did the Mock Turtle mean by
8   Ambition?
9   Distraction?
10 Uglification?
11 Derision?
12 What word in the passage means "a half-witted person?"

(B) *Cue for Treason*, by Geoffrey Trease.
    This is a story of Elizabethan England which is often read in schools. Read the following extract about London at that time and then answer the questions.

    Not that London wasn't a grand place then, with Christmas coming, and the Lord Chamberlain's Men commanded to act before the Queen at Court on Twelfth Night. That was the climax of a fortnight's hard work and festivities: when we weren't acting to crammed, good-natured audiences, we were enjoying ourselves at Shakespeare's place in Bishopsgate, or the Desmonds' rooms at the Flower de Luce, or skating on the ponds out Kensington way. But I shall never forget Twelfth Night at Whitehall Palace, with our stage set in the great hall. It was all hung with holly and ivy and bays and rosemary and mistletoe, and a thousand candles winking on the ladies' jewels, and the Queen sitting just in front of us, her silken skirts curving out around her like a cascade of silver, her great ruff framing her face like a halo. . . . We did Shakespeare's *Merry Wives of Windsor*, which he had written to please her, because she wanted to see the fat man, Falstaff, in love. Kit was Anne Page and I was Mistress Quickly. Several times I made the Queen herself laugh right out loud. We got ten pounds for the whole show, which was good but nothing extraordinary. The Queen was very economical, and felt that we really ought to be satisfied with the advertisement we got through being her favourite actors. It didn't make any difference to us apprentices, anyhow; what pleased us was the marvellous food they gave us, dishes left over from the banquet—roast peacock and swan, buttered oranges, tansy, and "snow", which was mostly cream, sugar, and white of egg, and slipped down very pleasantly when we were stuffed with the heavier things. It's true I was rather ill during the night afterwards, and Kit called me a fat Christmas hog, but it was worth it.

1   Why was London a grand place just then?
2   Where was Shakespeare's place in London?
3   What famous Palace is mentioned?
4   What play was acted before the Queen?
5   How was the stage decorated?
6   What three characters are mentioned as occurring in the play?
7   How much did the actors get for the whole show?
8   When is Twelfth Night?

    What words in the passage mean:
9   A kind of starched collar often worn in Tudor times?
10 Pouring down like a torrent?

(C) *Moonfleet*, by J. Meade Falkner.
     **This is a thrilling story about smugglers of the eighteenth century. It has been read by thousands of school-children and although first published in 1898, is still as popular as ever.
     Read this extract about how John Trenchard and his companion descended into the cave.**

> The stairs were still sharp cut and little worn, but Elzevir paid great care to his feet, lest he should slip on the ferns and mosses with which they were overgrown. When we reached the brambles he met them with his back, and though I heard the thorns tearing in his coat, he shoved them aside with his broad shoulders, and screened my dangling leg from getting caught. Thus he came without stumble to the bottom of the pit.
> When we got there all was dark, but he stepped off into a narrow opening on the right hand, and walked on as if he knew the way. I could see nothing, but perceived that we were passing through endless galleries cut in the solid rock, high enough, for the most part, to allow of walking upright, but sometimes so low as to force him to bend down and carry me in a very constrained attitude. Only twice did he set me down at a turning, while he took out his tinder-box and lit a match; but at length the dark-

ness became less dark, and I saw that we were in a large cave or room, into which the light came through some opening at the far end. At the same time I felt a colder breath and fresh salt smell in the air that told me we were very near the sea.

Now answer these questions:—

1   Why did Elzevir pay great care to his feet?
2   How did he meet the brambles?
3   Why did Elzevir carry John?
4   What did they pass through?
5   How many times did Elzevir light a match?
6   With what did he light the match?
7   From where did the light enter the cave?
8   How did John know that they were near the sea?

34

(A) Read the following passage from *Annapurna*, a 26,493 ft. mountain peak in the Himalayas, first climbed by a Frenchman, Maurice Herzog, in 1950.

The intense cold of this minute grotto shrivelled us up, the enclosing walls of ice were damp and the floor a fresh carpet of snow; by huddling together there was just room for the four of us. Icicles hung from the ceiling and we broke some of them off to make more head room and kept little bits to suck—it was a long time since we had had anything to drink.

That was our shelter for the night. At least we should be protected from the wind, and the temperature would remain fairly even, though the damp was extremely unpleasant. We settled ourselves in the dark as best we could. As always in a bivouac, we took off our boots; without this precaution the constriction would cause immediate frostbite. Terray unrolled the sleeping-bag which he had had the foresight to bring, and settled himself in relative comfort. We put on everything warm that we had, and to avoid contact with the snow I sat on the cine-camera. We huddled close up to each other, in our search for a hypothetical position in which the warmth of all bodies should be combined without loss, but we could not keep still for a second.

Now answer these questions:—

1 What do you think is meant by 'a minute grotto'?
2 Of what were the walls made?
3 Why did they break off the icicles from the ceiling?
4 What did they do to prevent immediate frostbite?
5 Who slept in comparative comfort and why?
6 How many men were there?
7 To avoid contact with the snow what did the writer do?
8 What did they all try to do?
9 What is the noun formed from the adjective "hypothetical"?
10 Give the noun formed from the verb "protected".

(B) Read the following from a novel called *Woodstock*, by Sir Walter Scott (1771-1832). It is about Puritan soldiers of the Civil Wars 1642-51.

The elder amongst them sat or lay on the benches, with their high steeple-crowned hats pulled over their severe and knitted brows, waiting for the Presbyterian parson, as mastiffs sit in dumb expectation of the bull that is to be brought to the stake. The younger mixed, some of them, a bolder license of manners with their heresies; they gazed round on the women, yawned, coughed, and whispered, ate apples, and cracked nuts, as if in the gallery of a theatre ere the piece commences.

Besides all these, the congregation contained a few soldiers, some in corselets and steel caps, some in buff, and others in red coats. These men of war had their bandoliers, with ammunition, slung round them, and rested on their pikes and muskets. They, too, had their peculiar doctrines on the most difficult points of religion, and united the extravagances of enthusiasm with the most determined courage and resolution in the field. The burghers of Woodstock looked on these military saints with no small degree of awe; for though not often sullied with deeds of plunder or cruelty, they had the power of both absolutely in their hands, and the peaceful citizens had no alternative save submission to whatever the ill-regulated and enthusiastic imaginations of their martial guides might suggest.

Now answer these questions:—

1. What kind of hats did the older people wear?
2. From their behaviour, where might the younger people have been?
3. What word leads you to suppose that all these people were in church?
4. How were the soldiers dressed?
5. What weapons did they carry?
6. How would you say they behaved in battle?
7. How did the citizens regard them?
8. In your notebooks write TRUE or FALSE for the following statements:—
    (a) All the soldiers wore red coats.
    (b) They did not often plunder the citizens.
    (c) The citizens had to submit to the soldiers.
    (d) The younger people were well-behaved in church.
9. What rather cruel sport is referred to here?
10. Give the *verb* formed from the noun "resolution".

(C) The following is about *Rip Van Winkle* by an American writer, Washington Irving (1783-1859). Rip is supposed to have gone to sleep for a great many years and on waking to have visited his native village where he found everything had altered beyond recognition. Read the passage and then answer the questions that follow.

There was as usual, a crowd of folks about the door, but none that Rip recollected. The very character of the people seemed changed. There was a busy, bustling, disputatious tone about it, instead of the accustomed phlegm and drowsy tranquillity.

The appearance of Rip, with his long grizzled beard, his rusty fowling-piece, his uncouth dress, and an army of women and children at his heels, soon attracted attention. The tavern politicians crowded round him, eyeing him from head to foot with great curiosity. A knowing, self-important old gentleman, in a sharp cocked hat, made his way through the crowd, putting them to the right and left with his elbows as he passed, and planting himself before Van Winkle, with one arm akimbo, the other resting on his cane, his keen eyes and sharp hat penetrating, as it were, into his very soul, demanded in an austere tone: "What brought him to the election with a gun on his shoulder and a mob at his heels, and whether he meant to breed a riot in the village?"—"Alas! gentlemen", cried Rip, somewhat dismayed, "I am a poor quiet man, a native of the place, and a loyal subject of the king, God bless him!"

Here a general shout burst from the bystanders: "A tory! a tory! a spy! a refugee! hustle him! away with him!" It was with great difficulty that the self-important man in the cocked hat restored ·order; and he demanded again of the unknown culprit what he came there for, and for whom he was seeking? The poor man humbly assured him that he meant no harm, but merely came there in search of some of his neighbours, who used to keep about the tavern.

1 How did the character of the people seem changed?
2 What was there strange about the appearance of Rip?
3 Who followed him?
4 Who especially crowded round him?
5 What was happening in the village when Rip entered it?
6 What did they think that Rip intended to do?
7 What did the bystanders think he was?
8 What did Rip tell them he came in search of?
9 From the passage name:
   (a) an adjective describing Rip's beard.
   (b) a noun which means 'quietness'.
   (c) two proper nouns.
   (d) a noun meaning the name of a political party.

35

(A) *Tom Brown's Schooldays,* by Thomas Hughes (1822-96).
This famous school story deals with life at Rugby in the nineteenth century. The following passage describes a boy's study.

It wasn't very large certainly, being about six feet long by four broad. It couldn't be called light, as there were bars and a grating to the window; which little precautions were necessary in the studies on the groundfloor, looking out into the close, to prevent the exit of small boys after locking-up, and the entrance of contraband articles. But it was uncommonly comfortable to look at, Tom thought. The space under the window at the farther end was occupied by a square table covered with a reasonably clean and whole red and blue check tablecloth; a hard-seated sofa covered with red stuff occupied one side, running up to the end, and making a seat for one, or by sitting close, for two, at the table; and a good stout wooden chair afforded a seat to another boy, so that three could sit and work together. The walls were wainscoted half-way up; the wainscot being covered with green baize, the remainder with a bright-patterned paper, on which hung three or four prints of dogs' heads, Grimaldi winning the Aylesbury steeple-chase, Amy Robsart, the reigning Waverley beauty of the day, and Tom Crib in a posture of defence, which did no great credit to the science of that hero, if truly represented. Over the door were a row of hat-pegs, and on each side bookcases with cupboards at the bottom; shelves and cupboards being filled indiscriminately with school-books, a cup or two, a mouse-trap and brass candlesticks, leather straps, a fustian bag, and some curious-looking articles, which puzzled Tom not a little, until his friend explained that they were climbing-irons, and showed their use. A cricket-bat and small fishing rod stood up in one corner.

Now answer the following:—

1 What were the dimensions of the study?
2 Why did the windows have bars and a grating?
3 What did Tom think of the study?
4 How many boys could sit in the study?

5 Of whom was the picture of the boxer?
6 Mention any two items of furniture contained in the study.
7 Another picture was of a jockey. Who was he?
8 What were there on each side of the door?
9 What curious-looking articles puzzled Tom?
10 What two articles are connected with sport?

(B) *Memoirs of a Mountaineer,* by F. Spencer Chapman.

F. Spencer Chapman was a schoolmaster who turned to the hazardous pastime of mountaineering and during the Second World War was specially selected by the War Office to train a ski battalion. His *Memoirs* make fascinating reading and his assault on the 20,000 feet Tibetan peak Chomolhari with only one porter was a wonderful feat of endurance and skill. The following passage describes some of the equipment carried by the climbers during the ascent of Chomolhari in May, 1937.

May 20th dawned superlatively fine. I got up at 3 o'clock and made porridge and tea for breakfast. Kikuli was quite cheerful at the prospect of getting off the mountain and said he was capable of leading. Crawford, on the other hand, was feeling little better, but was sure he would recover once he was lower down. We had much sorting of gear to do before we could start, and as the two tents were frozen into the snow, it was not until 5.30 that we parted company. Pasang and I took one rucksack each, our ice-axes, a 100-foot rope, the better bivouac tent, two pitons, a double eiderdown sleeping bag each, and a small li-lo, my Contax camera and telephoto lens, a primus, a cooking-pot, mugs, plates, spoons, two boxes of matches and a tin-opener. For food we took three tins of sardines, a tongue and a tin of herrings, two pounds of pemmican, threequarters of a pound of sweets, four half-pound slabs of chocolate, some oatmeal, sugar, butter, tea and pulled bread. Pasang also brought a bag of "tsambo" and a brick of Tibetan tea. I wore my felt-lined climbing boots, four pairs of ordinary socks, cotton pants, shorts, grey flannel trousers, a flannel shirt, a high-necked jersey with sleeves and a smaller sleeveless pullover, an imitation-leather wind-jacket (this had a zip-fastener which had gone wrong, and was attached with safety-pins), a single Grenfell-cloth windproof suit with a fur-edged hood, wool mitts, horse-leather mitts, a balaclava wool helmet, and snow glasses. Of medical supplies we took only a tube of Anti-Lux, some sticking-plaster and an envelope of aspirins. Although we hoped to be off the snow in a couple of days, this outfit was designed to last us for as much as a week in case of necessity. We were carrying about 20 lb. each.

Now answer the following:—

1 What sort of day did May 20th promise to be?
2 How was Kikuli feeling?
3 When did Crawford think he would be feeling better?
4 How long were they before parting company?
5 What two sleeping items did Pasang and the writer take with them?
6 What tinned food did they take with them?
7 What did the writer wear on his feet?
8 What medical supplies did they carry?
9 For how long was the total outfit designed to last?
10 What weight did each man carry?

(C) *Far from the Madding Crowd*, **by Thomas Hardy (1840-1928).**
Many novelists are identified with various parts of the country, such as Arnold Bennett with the Potteries, Hugh Walpole with Cumberland, Phyllis Bentley with Yorkshire, Sheila Kaye-Smith with Sussex, and so on. Thomas Hardy is one of the greatest of these regional novelists. The county of Dorset is the "Wessex" of his novels. He writes about country folk and scenes. *Far From the Madding Crowd* **first appeared in 1874. Here the author describes**

FARMER OAK

When Farmer Oak smiled, the corners of his mouth spread till they were within an unimportant distance of his ears, his eyes were reduced to chinks, and diverging wrinkles appeared round them, extending upon his countenance like the rays in a rudimentary sketch of the rising sun.

His Christian name was Gabriel, and on working days he was a young man of sound judgment, easy notions, proper dress, and general good character. On Sundays he was a man of misty views, rather given to postponing, and hampered by his best clothes and umbrella: upon the whole, one who felt himself to occupy morally that vast middle space of Laodicean neutrality which lay between the Communion people of the parish and the drunken section,—that is, he went to church, but yawned privately by the time the congregation reached the Nicene creed, and thought of what there would be for dinner when he meant to be listening to the sermon. Or, to state his character as it stood in the scale of public opinion, when his friends and critics were in tantrums, he was considered rather a bad man; when they were pleased, he was rather a good man; when they were neither, he was a man whose moral colour was a kind of pepper-and-salt mixture.

Since he lived six times as many working-days as Sundays, Oak's appearance in his old clothes was most peculiarly his own —the mental picture formed by his neighbours in imagining him being always dressed in that way. He wore a low-crowned felt hat, spread out at the base by tight jamming upon the head for security in high winds, and a coat like Dr. Johnson's; his lower extremities being encased in ordinary leather leggings and boots emphatically large, affording to each foot a roomy apartment so constructed that any wearer might stand in a river all day long and know nothing of damp—their maker being a conscientious man who endeavoured to compensate for any weekness in his cut by unstinted dimension and solidity.

Answer the following:—

1. What was Farmer Oak's Christian name?
2. Was he an old or a young man?
3. When he smiled, something appeared rather small, and something else rather large. What were they?
4. When was he given to putting off things?
5. What did he often think of during the sermon?

6   What did his friends think of him when they were in a bad mood?
7   Why did he jam his hat tightly upon his head?
8   What kind of boots did he wear?
9   What did he have round his legs?
10 A young child often has these. What are they? The word is mentioned in the passage.

36

(A) *Beyond the Burma Road,* by Percy F. Westerman.
Percy F. Westerman is a well-known writer of boys' books. He has published over 150 of them and they have been translated into French, Dutch, Danish, Norwegian Swedish, Polish and Hungarian, so that other boys besides English read them. The following extract comes from *Beyond the Burma Road.*

AMBUSHED BY DACOITS

The train had run into a Dacoit ambush. Fortunately the line was now in a fairly flat district with jungle on either side. The bandits had derailed the engine and four carriages by unbolting a section of the metals.

Dacoitry had been a popular means of gain to the savage tribes of Upper Burma until the British took over the country in 1895. Even so it had taken them several years before dacoitry had been stamped out—permanently it had been hoped. But in yet another of many ways, the results of Burma's independence quickly manifested itself. Murder and pillage by armed bands of robbers were already rampant.

Keith was told to leave the carriage with the other passengers, none of whom had been injured in the telescoped part of the train. This, he realized, was an occasion when it would have been fatal for him to use his revolver, for even before alighting he found himself covered by the rifles of half a dozen ferocious bandits.

He took advantage of the confusion to drop his pistol and ammunition on the floor under the seat. There was a chance of their being unnoticed.

The passengers were lined up well clear of the derailed carriages, while about a dozen Dacoits kept them covered. Keith noticed that the armed men carried not less than five different types of rifles. He could recognize the British Lee-Enfield, the American .300, and the Jap small-bore. The others, which he could not place, were German and Dutch. He wondered how they were off for ammunition for such a variety of weapons.

A couple of ferocious-looking bandits, evidently the chief and the second-in-command, appeared and ordered the passengers to produce their money and valuables and place them on the ground.

Answer the following:—

1 In what sort of district did the ambush occur?
2 How did the bandits derail the train?
3 When did the British first take over Upper Burma?
4 What was one result of Burma's independence?
5 What was Keith told to do?
6 What did he do during the confusion?
7 About how many bandits kept the passengers covered?
8 How many different types of rifles did they have?
9 What two types of rifles were unrecognized by Keith?
10 What did the bandits order the passengers to do?

(B) *My Early Life*, by Winston S. Churchill.

Few men have had a more adventurous life than Sir Winston Churchill. When he was a very young man he went as a War Correspondent of *The Morning Post* to South Africa during the Boer War. An armoured train in which he was travelling was derailed and attacked but Mr. Churchill, as he then was, took charge of the defence. He was, however, captured by the Boers but afterwards escaped. The Boers offered £25 for his capture "dead or alive".

The following extract tells of his capture at the time of the attack on the armoured train on November 15th, 1899. His captor was General Louis Botha, a famous Boer leader.

Fifty yards away was a small platelayer's cabin of masonry: there was cover there. About 200 yards away was the rocky gorge of the Blue Krantz River: there was plenty of cover there. I determined to make a dash for the river. I rose to my feet. Suddenly on the other side of the railway, separated from me by the rails and two uncut wire fences, I saw a horseman galloping furiously, a tall, dark figure, holding his rifle in his right hand. He pulled up his horse almost in its own length and shaking the rifle at me shouted a loud command. We were forty yards apart. That morning I had taken with me, Correspondent-status notwithstanding, my Mauser pistol. I thought I could kill this man, and after the treatment had received I earnestly desired to do so. I put my hand to my belt, the pistol was not there. When engaged in clearing the line, getting in and out of the engine, etc., I had taken it off. It came safely home on the engine. I have it now! But at this moment I was quite unarmed. Meanwhile, I suppose in about the time this takes to tell, the Boer horseman, still seated on his horse, had covered me with his rifle. The animal stood stock still, so did he, and so did I. I looked towards the river, I looked towards the platelayer's hut. The Boer continued to look along his sights. I thought there was absolutely no chance of escape, if he fired he would surely hit me, so I held up my hands and surrendered myself as a prisoner of war.

Now answer these questions:—

1 Of what was the platelayer's cabin made?
2 Why did Mr. Churchill decide to make for the river?
3 What separated him from the horseman?
4 How far apart were the two men?
5 What had happened to Mr. Churchill's pistol?
6 What kind was it?
7 Why should he not have carried a pistol?
8 Why did Mr. Churchill surrender?
9 What do we call the story of one's life such as this and indeed in the following extract where the life story is related by the person concerned?

(C) *Coco the Clown*, by Himself.

Nicolai Poliakoff, who wrote this book, was born in 1900 in Russia. From the very first he determined to be a circus "artiste". He ran away from home but came back and was beaten by his father. He rigged up a stage in his back-yard and gave shows to children of the neighbourhood for a small charge. He eventually joined a circus with his father's consent and finally became one of the most famous clowns in the world. Coco has performed at Bellevue, Manchester, and in Bertram Mills's Circus at Olympia. The following extract describes his first visit to a circus.

I sat with mouth open, amazed and delighted. This was the most wonderful thing that had ever happened to me. I was so awed that I forgot to applaud the turns. There were jugglers, girls on horseback, trapeze artistes, tumblers, all the things that go to make the circus the most popular attraction in the world. I forgot that I was a small, homeless boy, with nowhere to sleep; forgot everything except that I was seeing a circus.

Suddenly a loud noise from the band awakened me from my dreams. Looking up, I saw that the ring was empty. The ring master was announcing: 'Lazerenko. The most famous clown in all the Russias'.

Before he had finished speaking I thought that Lazerenko must be the most famous clown in all the world. But I couldn't see him.

Suddenly he appeared on top of the bandstand. With a shout he dived headlong down into the ring. He was followed by a seemingly endless stream of old pots and pans, which made an ear-splitting clatter as they crashed into the ring. Lazerenko sat amongst these with such a pained expression on his comical face, that the circus rocked with laughter. But I didn't laugh. I was wondering how he managed to fall so far without hurting himself.

I cannot remember all the things he did, but I know he gave a wonderful exhibition of clowning. When it was over I made up my mind that I was going to be a clown and nothing else.

Answer the following:—

1 What did Coco forget to do?
2 How is the circus described?

3 Mention any two types of performers Coco saw at the circus.
4 What awakened him from his dreams?
5 How was Lazerenko announced?
6 Where did he first appear?
7 What made a din?
8 What puzzled Coco?
9 Where are two very famous circuses held in England?

37

(A) *In Search of England*, by H. V. Morton.
This is a description of a journey by car around England which was first published in 1927. In the following extract, the writer describes his visit to Salisbury.

I had two great moments in Salisbury. It was market day. The cattle market was loud with mooing and bleating. Country gigs stood in the square and over the pens leaned the burly, red-faced Wiltshire farmers. Many a Tess went off, with a basket over her arm to buy—lisle-thread stockings, I suppose. I looked at the crowd and heard their bargaining. I met them in Ox Row and Blue Boar Row and Oatmeal Row. I watched them come from tap-rooms wiping their mouths with the backs of their big hands and—the railway might never have invaded Salisbury.

The other moment? It was evening and the sun was setting behind the cathedral. In that walled close nothing it seemed could ever hurt: the soft green grass, the mighty church pointing its slim finger to the sky, and the old grey cloistered buildings dedicated to centuries of peace. I went inside. It is not, to my mind, one of the loveliest of our cathedrals, but it is one of the most chastely dignified; it sings on the same note. St. Paul's in London, Truro Cathedral, and Salisbury Cathedral, stand alone, I think, as the work of one generation. . . .

A little whisper of organ music lost itself in the grey arches. When it was dark I visited the old inns of Salisbury and walked through quiet streets which are the streets of Barchester.

Now answer these questions.

1 What was being held in Salisbury when the writer visited it?
2 What is a "country gig"?
3 In what county is Salisbury?
4 What did the writer suppose many of the women were buying?
5 Three streets are named here. What are they?
6 What sort of spire has Salisbury Cathedral would you imagine from this description?
7 What two other cathedrals were probably built about the same time according to the writer?
8 What are cloisters?
9 What did the writer think about the cathedral—that it was very ugly, beautiful, dignified?
10 What did he hear inside the cathedral?

(B) *The Cloister and the Hearth,* **by Charles Reade.**

Charles Reade (1814-84) was a Victorian novelist who wrote various stories about social abuses of his day. It's Never Too Late to Mend **deals with the prison system,** Hard Cash **with the evils of private lunatic asylums, and** Foul Play **with the danger of overloaded ships.** The Cloister and the Hearth **is a fine and exciting story of the Middle Ages. The following extract tells us of the ingenious way in which Gerard escaped from prison.**

As the sun declined, Gerard's heart too sank and sank; with the waning light even the embers of hope went out. He sat upon the chest, his arms and his head drooping before him, a picture of despondency. Suddenly something struck the wall beyond him very sharply, and then rattled on the floor at his feet. It was an arrow; he saw the white feather. He crouched. No more missiles came. He crawled on all fours, and took up the arrow; there was no head to it. He took it up, and felt it all over: he found a soft substance attached to it. His tinder-box enabled him to strike a light: it showed him two things that made his heart bound with delight, none the less thrilling for being somewhat vague. Attached to the arrow was a skein of silk, and on the arrow itself were words written.

"Well-beloved, make fast the silk to thy knife and lower to us: but hold thine end fast: then count an hundred and draw up."

Gerard seized the oak chest, and dragged it to the window. Standing on it and looking down, he saw figures at the tower foot. He waved his bonnet to them with trembling hand: then he undid the silk rapidly but carefully, and made one end fast to his knife and lowered it till it ceased to draw. Then he counted a hundred. Then pulled the silk carefully up: it came up a little heavier. At last he came to a large knot, and by that knot a stout whipcord was attached to the silk. Margaret's voice came up to him, low but clear. 'Draw up, Gerard, till you see liberty.' At the word Gerard drew the whipcord line up, and drew and drew till he came to another knot, and found a cord of some thickness take the place of the whipcord. The weight got heavier and heavier, and at last he was well-nigh exhausted; looking down, he saw in the moonlight a sight that revived him: a stout new rope touched his hand: he hauled and hauled, and dragged the end into his prison, and instantly passed it through both handles of the chest in succession, and knotted it firmly, then sat for a moment to recover his breath and collect his courage.

Now answer these questions:—

1 What did Charles Reade mainly write about and in what period did he live?
2 When the sun went down, what were Gerard's feelings?
3 What would he probably think when he first saw the arrow?
4 What was there fastened to the arrow?
5 What was he told to do with it?
6 What was there fastened to the thinnest material?
7 How did he strike a light?
8 Why was he nearly exhausted?
9 To what did he fasten the rope?

10 What word in the passage means
    (a) Something which is shot or fired?
    (b) Very down-hearted?

(C) **Sir Henry Rider Haggard (1856-1925) wrote many interesting novels such as** *She, Nada the Lily,* **and** *Allan Quartermain.* *King Solomon's Mines,* **from which the following extract is taken, was written in nine days, so it was something of a "nine days' wonder". The passage describes the meeting of Allan Quartermain, Sir Henry Curtis and Captain John Good, with the Kukuanas.**

"How is it, O strangers", asked the old man solemnly, "that this fat man (pointing to Good, who was clad in nothing but boots and flannel shirt, and had only half finished his shaving), whose body is clothed, and whose legs are bare, who grows hair on one side of his sickly face and not on the other, and who wears one shining and transparent eye—how is it, I ask, that he has teeth which move of themselves, coming away from the jaws and returning of their own will?"

"Open your mouth", I said to Good, who promptly curled up his lips and grinned at the old gentleman like an angry dog, revealing to his astonished gaze two thin red lines of gum as utterly innocent of ivories as a new-born elephant. The audience gasped.

"Where are his teeth?" they shouted: "with our eyes we saw them."

Turning his head slowly and with a gesture of ineffable contempt, Good swept his hand across his mouth. Then he grinned again, and lo, there were two rows of lovely teeth.

Now the young man who had flung the knife threw himself down on the grass and gave vent to a prolonged howl of terror; and as for the old gentleman, his knees knocked together with fear.

"I see that ye are spirits", he said falteringly; "did ever man born of woman have hair on one side of his face and not on the other, or a round and transparent eye, or teeth which moved and melted away and grew again? Pardon us, O my lords."

Answer these questions:—

1. What had Good only half-finished?
2. What did the old man mean when he said that Good wore "one shining and transparent eye"?
3. What did Good do to frighten the audience?
4. Who probably were the Kukuanas—gentlemen, Englishmen, savages, Bedouins?
5. What leads one to suppose that the speaker, Allan Quartermain, was an elephant hunter?
6. What did the old gentleman think the strangers were?
7. What did the young man who had flung the knife do?
8. What words in the passage mean
    (a) Too great for words, unutterable?
    (b) Something that can be seen through?

38

(A) **The following extract is taken from a book called *Out With Romany*, by G. Bramwell Evens, and describes a fight between Hotchi and an adder.**

As I spoke, the hedgehog rushed swiftly at the snake, and as she neared him pulled down her front spines over her face.

The snake struck at her nose with an angry hiss, then recoiled quickly as his own nose got the sharp pricks of Hotchi's bristles. Quick as lightning, Hotchi uncovered her head for a second, and before the snake could recover, she had seized it by the tail and curled herself up into a spiny ball. Again and again the snake struck savagely at the prickly ball, each time wounding himself more severely. Hotchi remained curled up, holding on grimly to the tail, until the snake grew more and more feeble and lay exhausted. Then, and not till then, did Hotchi relax her hold.

"She's chewing the snake's tail!" Tim whispered excitedly.

"She's going to make a meal of him", I said, as we watched the snake disappearing. When the hedgehog had eaten half of it, she paused, looked round, and shuffled off without giving another glance at the victim.

"She has had enough", I said. "She'll go back to her hole and have a good sleep. What with frogs, and half an adder, she must be about full up."

When the hedgehog had disappeared, we walked over to the scene of the combat. I picked up the remains.

"Be careful, Romany", whispered Tim fearfully.

"It's all right, Tim. I wanted to show you the V plainly marked behind the head. We'll have a look at his mouth." I prised it open with my knife, inserting a twig into the open jaws.

Now answer the following:—

1 What did the hedgehog do when it approached the snake?
2 What did the snake do when Hotchi approached?
3 What part of the snake did the hedgehog seize?
4 How much of the snake did the hedgehog eat?
5 What else do hedgehogs eat?
6 How would you distinguish an adder?
7 Why did Romany insert a twig into the open jaws of the adder?

(B) This passage is taken from *Farmer's Glory*, by A. G. Street, a well-known broadcaster and writer on farming. It tells how Granfer proved to be right about the hens after all.

Next morning after breakfast Granfer struggled out of bed. Mary, surprised to hear the noise, ran upstairs to find the old chap getting into his clothes. 'Feyther', she cried. 'Whatever be you a doing? You get back to bed.'

'Thee find me boots', ordered Granfer. 'I be gwaine out. 'Tis come at last.'

'What be come?'

'T' water, ye vooil. Cassn't yer thic rumblen'? 'Tis awver Bickton Mill, I tell 'ee. 'Elp I downstairs, an get me boots.'

'But you musn't, Feyther. Doctor said as 'ow—'

'Dang the girl. I tell 'ee I be gwaine out. Zummut's up! Come on, oot.'

Unwillingly Mary obeyed, and Granfer toiled downstairs, and struggled into his boots. 'Now, 'elp I on wie me coat, an' gie I me sticks.' Mary did so, and Granfer tottered outside for the first time for eight weeks.

He toiled up the lane with difficulty. When he reached his favourite spot by the farm-yard wall, he looked down on the Alder Plot. It was a scene of devastation. Some fowl houses were floating in the flood, and most of the remainder were leaning drunkenly at all angles. Dead and drowning fowls were being swept away, and in the midst of the maelstrom, he spied the General and a gardener trying to rescue some of the hens.

Granfer gazed on the scene for a few moments in silent satisfaction. Presently he saw Bill Yates and another man hurrying towards him.

'Hoy!' he yelled, waving one of his sticks in triumph. 'I telled un. I telled un. Wot about it now? Zilly owd vooil. Look at they hens. I knowed I wor right. Ho! Ho! Ho! Nackernism I be. Hoy! General!'

Here he turned and waved his stick at the General. Suddenly he stumbled, and fell to the ground. When Bill Yates and his companion reached him they thought he was dead.

'Poor wold feller', murmured Bill. "Twer too much fer un. He be gone, zur, I'm thinking.' This last to the General, who by that time had joined them.

They carried him gently down the lane to his cottage, and laid him on the sofa in the front room. As they looked at his withered old figure on the couch, his eyes opened. His gaze wandered vacantly round the room, but lighted up as he recognized the General. "Tis a pity about they hens, General', he mumbled, 'but I wor right. I be 'appier now in me mind.'

And then he died.

As the desire to be proved right in one's prophecies is one of the strongest forces in human nature, it would seem fairly certain that Granfer died 'appy.

Answer the following:—

1 What did Granfer demand first of all?

2 Certain words in this passage are in dialect. What is meant by the words "gwaine" and "vooil"?

3 For how long had Granfer probably been in bed?
4 Where was his favourite spot?
5 What word in this passage means 'a kind of whirlpool'?
6 What happened to most of the chickens?
7 To whom did they belong?
8 What were Granfer's feelings as he gazed on the scene?
9 What happened to him as a result?
10 What is one of the strongest forces in human nature?

(C) **The following extract is about *Volcanoes*. Read it and then answer the questions.**

A volcano is an opening in the earth's surface through which are erupted steam, gases, molten rock, dust, ashes, and other liquid and solid matter. The accumulation of material around the vent gives to the volcano its typical cone-like shape. The *neck*, through which materials are ejected, may be compared to the stem of a funnel leading to the bowl forming the *crater*.

Some volcanoes are built up almost entirely of cooled lava; others mainly of solidified ash, called *tuff*, and other fragmentary matter thrown out during an eruption. But the majority of cones consist of alternate layers of lava and tuff. Subsidiary cones are often formed at the sides of the volcano. Sometimes the crater becomes blocked up with solidified lava and ultimately the enormous pressure inside blows a portion of the mountain away. This happened in the case of Vesuvius, which is merely the remains of a much greater volcano known as Somma, a large part of which was blown away in the historic eruption of A.D. 79, when Herculaneum and Pompeii were both buried beneath clouds of volcanic ash.

1 What makes a volcano cone-like in shape?
2 What is the crater of a volcano?
3 What is the cooled substance called which is erupted from a volcano?
4 What is the solidified ash called?

5 When the crater becomes blocked, what sometimes may happen?
6 What particular mountain is an example of this?
7 What two cities were buried when this volcano erupted and when did it occur?
8 Where were these two cities situated?

39

(A) Read this extract:

THE ANNUAL SHOW

Every year during the first week of September, the inhabitants of Maxfield look forward to the Agricultural Show which takes place in the South Park.

Much careful planning and organisation is carried out by a special committee, and the preparations take place long beforehand, and the Borough Architect is responsible for the lay-out of the ground.

A team of men spend many days erecting the stands for the horse-jumping events. Soon, large marquees and numerous smaller tents spring up like mushrooms over-night.

On the day itself, huge crowds begin to make their way to the turnstiles, passing through a large space allotted to caravans and horse-boxes which have come from a great distance.

On the right as one enters, there is a fun-fair. Straight ahead is a slight eminence which has been enclosed for the horse-jumping events, with one side completely taken up by the grand stand which will hold about a thousand spectators. A children's gymkhana is held in the afternoon, and jumping events by adult riders from 6 p.m. till 8.30 p.m.

The horticultural exhibits are housed in two huge marquees. These comprise colourful displays of roses, dahlias, chrysanthemums, gladioli, and wonderful specimens of vegetables and fruit of every kind, and sometimes 'freak' specimens are to be seen, or some strange exotic plant.

The Women's Institutes from the surrounding districts vie with each other for the best exhibits of embroidery, table-decorations, cookery of all kinds, bottled fruits, jam, marmalade, and lemon-curd.

The cattle judging takes place in the morning and the trusses of hay, and tanks of water show that the welfare of the animals is catered for.

Sheep dog trials on a small scale are held on the west side of the show.

Every kind of agricultural machinery is displayed at the various stands on the entire western side of the ground and burly red-faced farmers are to be seen examining the latest make of tractor with a critical eye.

Rabbits, dogs, and birds are shown in their own marquees.

Refreshments are obtainable at all times of the day and schoolchildren are to be seen eating ice-cream, sucking candyfloss, and the like, while a special tent is set apart for the serving of meals.

Various local industries are represented such as gas, electricity, stone-masonry, and forestry, and there are many trade stands exhibiting special brands of food.

Schoolchildren send in specimens of arts and crafts and arrangements of wild flowers.

All money transactions are dealt with by travelling Banks which have their own caravans on the north side of the show ground.

As dusk approaches, a grand firework display takes place in a special enclosure by the lake, and now most of the other attractions are deserted and everybody flocks to see the 'set pieces'.

At 9.30 p.m. the show is over.

Now answer the following questions:—

1 Where is the show ground situated?
2 What are 'turnstiles'?
3 Who is responsible for the lay-out of the ground?
4 What do the Women's Institutes contribute to the show?
5 What does one see on the right as one enters the show ground?
6 What is a 'gymkhana'?

7   Why do you think the main jumping events take place in the evening?
8   How are the cattle cared for?
9   Which marquee would you visit if you were hungry?
10 What would you expect to find in the schoolchildren's section?
11 Name any piece of machinery you might see which could be used on a farm.
12 What exhibits would you find in the marquee devoted to 'Electricity'?
13 What animals would you expect to see in the pet show?
14 What activity is taking place on the west side of the show ground?
15 What is meant by 'travelling Banks'?
16 What is the final attraction of the show?

(B) Read the following extract from *The First Men in the Moon*, by H. G. Wells.

So we two poor terrestrial castaways, lost in that wild-growing moon jungle, crawled in terror before the sounds that had come upon us. We crawled as it seemed a long time before we saw either Selenite or mooncalf, though we heard the bellowing and gruntulous noises of these latter continually drawing nearer to us. We crawled through stony ravines, over snow slopes, amidst fungi that ripped like thin bladders at our thrust, emitting a watery humour; over a perfect pavement of things like puff-balls and beneath interminable thickets of scrub. And ever more hopelessly our eyes sought for our abandoned sphere. The noise of the mooncalves would at times be a vast, flat, calf-like sound, at times it rose to an amazed and wrathy bellowing, and again it would become a clogged, bestial sound as though these unseen creatures had sought to eat and bellow at the same time.

Our first view was but an inadequate, transitory glimpse, yet none the less disturbing because it was incomplete. Cavor was crawling in front at the time, and he first was aware of their proximity. He stopped, arresting me with a single gesture.

A crackling and smashing of the scrub appeared to be advancing directly upon us, and then, as we squatted close and endeavoured to judge of the nearness and direction of this noise, there came a terrific bellow behind us, so close and vehement that the tops of the bayonet scrub bent before it, and one felt the breath of it hot and moist. Turning about we saw indistinctly through a crowd of swaying stems the mooncalf's shining sides and the long line of its back looming against the sky.

Answer the following:—

1. What does the word 'terrestrial' mean?
2. Where were the two men lost?
3. Why were they frightened?
4. What are 'fungi'? What did they do when touched, and what did they emit?
5. What were the two men looking for?
6. How would you describe the three types of noise made by the mooncalves?
7. Why was the first view of them disturbing?
8. What appeared to be directly advancing upon the men?
9. What did the terrific bellow do?
10. What did they first see of the mooncalf?

(A) *The Radio Times.* **Programme for April 15th, 1958.**

★ ★ ★

2.30 WATCH WITH MOTHER

For the Very Young
Andy Pandy

Maria Bird brings Andy to play with your children and invites them to join in songs and games

Audrey Atterbury
and Molly Gibson
pull the strings
Gladys Whitred sings the songs

Script, music, and setting
by Maria Bird
(A BBC television film)

2.45–3.30 MAINLY FOR WOMEN

Family Affairs

Problems of Living

The 'Family Affairs' panel of experts discuss problems sent by viewers

Dr. Winifred de Kok
Rose Hacker
The Rev. Walter Lane
James Hemming

In the chair,
Olive Shapley

Letters to the panel should be sent to 'Family Affairs', BBC Television Centre, London, W.12

Produced by BERYL RADLEY

3.15 Character and Handwriting

1—*Does it matter how you write?*
Joan Cambridge
explains why it does,
and introduces two personalities
to help illustrate the principles
of handwriting analysis
Produced by MONICA SIMS

5.0 CHILDREN'S TELEVISION

presents
'THE MACHINE BREAKERS'
A serial in three parts
by PHYLLIS BENTLEY

3—'The Trial'

Characters in order of appearance:

Will Oldroyd.................DAVID HIGSON
Dick Bamforth.............CAVAN KENDALL
Constable....................PETER HUGHES
Mr. Stancliffe...........JEFFERSON CLIFFORD
Tom Thorpe................PETER HAWKINS
George Mellor...............SIMON MERRICK
Benjamin Walker.........PATRICK WESTWOOD
Joe Bamforth............STUART HUTCHISON
Mary...........................ANNE REID
Clerk of the Court...............IVAN OWEN
Topping, Counsel for Prosecution
BRUNO BARNABE
Judge......................HAROLD YOUNG
Brougham, Counsel for Defence
ANTHONY MARLOWE
Foreman of Jury.............JOHN BARRETT

Film sequences by the
BBC television film unit
Produced by BARBARA HAMMOND
(Previously televised on June 2, 1957)

5.30 OUT OF DOORS

A monthly look
at the countryside

Bruce Campbell
introduces

The Month of April
What to look for
and how to find it

Eyes and Ears
Children from Bristol schools
compete in a quiz

Storyteller
Frank Sawyer, river-keeper

Badminton
A visit with Dorian Williams to the grounds of Badminton House where preparations are in full swing for the three-day Badminton Horse Trials.

Film commentary, Johnny Morris

Film Editor, Christopher Parsons
Produced by WINWOOD READE
From the BBC's
West of England studio

This is an extract of part of a programme from *The Radio Times*. Study it carefully and then answer these questions:—

1 Would you describe *The Radio Times* as a newspaper, magazine, or novel?
2 What is the programme called which is for very young people?
3 Who invites the children to join in songs and games?
4 Who is Andy Pandy, and how do you know?
5 Who sings the songs?
6 Who are the experts in the programme "Mainly for Women"?
7 What do they discuss?
8 In the programme, "Character and Handwriting", what is meant by 'personalities' and 'analysis'?
9 Who shows that it does matter how you write?
10 What is meant by 'a serial play'?
11 Who is the author of the serial play with which Children's Television opens?
12 What two characters in this play have the same surname?
13 What is another name for all the characters together in a play?
14 What do you understand by the 'Foreman of the Jury'?
15 Which programme contains a 'quiz'?
16 Who competes in this 'quiz'?
17 From which studio are the Badminton Horse Trials televised?

(B) Study this extract on SHOCK, from the *Handbook of the Royal Life Saving Society*, and then answer the questions.

The best method of treating shock is to conserve the heat of the body by using wrappings of any available material which should be applied closely and quickly underneath as well as above so that heat is not lost through the surface on which the patient is lying. Any artificial warmth which can be produced should be added—hot water in bags or bottles, hot bricks, bags of hot sand, or heated articles. The heat of each article should be carefully checked with the hand to make sure that it is not excessive; and at least one layer of cloth or several layers of paper should be placed between it and the patient. The articles should be placed in the armpits, between the thighs and along the sides of the trunk.

Although the treatment of shock is very important, the checking of severe bleeding and the administration of artificial respiration, if they be necessary, *should receive priority of treatment in that order*. Unconsciousness with breathing demands that the patient be placed comfortably on the back with the head turned fully to one side. Restrictive clothing should be loosened.

If breathing has ceased, artificial respiration must be commenced at once. If at the commencement a choice of position is possible, the patient should be placed with the head slightly, but not very much, downhill. A diagonal position on a fairly steep slope will lessen the actual slope of the patient.

1 Where must the wrappings be applied to conserve the heat of the patient's body?
2 What artificial warmth can be applied?
3 What should be done with each article before it is applied?
4 What should be placed between the article and the patient?
5 Where should these articles be placed?
6 What symptoms should receive priority of treatment?
7 If the patient is unconscious, in what position should he be placed?
8 If breathing has ceased, what treatment should be applied first?
9 What do you understand by
  (a) Excessive?
  (b) Artificial respiration?
  (c) Restrictive clothing?

40 COMPREHENSION EXERCISES IN ENGLISH

ANSWERS

R. E. HOUSEMAN
M.A., LONDON, M.ED., MANCHESTER

HULTON EDUCATIONAL
PUBLICATIONS

1

(A)
1 An inn.
2 A bay.
3 A sabre-cut cheek.
4 Road.
5 To his mother.
6 Robert Louis Stevenson.
7 Author.
8 Hulton Educational Publications Ltd.
9 135.

(B)
1 Crafty.
2 Devonshire.
3 Stags and hounds.
4 Nearly 800 yards.
5 Opposite.
6 The keeper, steward, gardener, ploughman, dairy maid.
7 A chase or pursuit.
8 He chuckled to himself merrily.

(C)
1 Thirteen.
2 Ten people.
3 Frank.
4 Farmer.
5 Thursday, 27th February.
6 7th March, 1945.
7 In the country.
8 Evening.
9 Niece.
10 Wednesday, 5th March.

2

(A)
1 A horse.
2 One who attends to the well-being of a horse.
3 Never did me any harm.
4 To keep them in good condition.
5 Its neck.
6 The bit.
7 The saddle.
8 The crupper.
9 A fraud.
10 An autobiography.

(B)
1 Dear.
2 Grateful.
3 Delightful.
4 Unhappy.
5 Welcome.
6 Cheerful or happy.
7 Sensible.
8 Kind.
9 Good-tempered.
10 Ever or always.

Any other suitable alternative should be accepted.

(C)
1 Mr. Brown.
2 Baby.
3 Billy.
4 Jill.
5 Tom.
6 Jill.

3

(A)
1 On a hill.
2 Wind.
3 To thresh corn.
4 Open.
5 Maize, wheat and rye.

(B)
1 The negro race.
2 Round and shining. Glittering as glass beads.
3 With astonishment at the wonders of the new mas'r's parlour.
4 White and brilliant.
5 Filthy and ragged.
6 A kind of sacking.
7 Odd and goblin - like, heathenish.
8 Master's.

(C)
1 Starlit and cool.
2 A suggestion of moisture, scent of wet earth and dripping leaves.
3 Along the Dover Road, for forty miles.
4 A pure strain of finely-bred horses.
5 Dexterous.
6 No.
7 Very infrequent comments.
8 What went on in that slow-going head of his.
9 (a) an adjective.
  (b) a verb.
  (c) a noun.
  (d) an adverb.
10 (a) masculine.
  (b) slowly.
  (c) always or ever.

4

(A)
1 Sprigged-muslin.
2 Apple-green velvet.
3 Jill.
4 Nigger-brown woollen material.

(B)
1 Recipe.
2 Ground ginger and mixed spice.
3 Flour, sugar, spice, or ground ginger.
4 Because they are most important.
5 Ounces.
6 Temperature must not be too high or too low.
7 Chopped lemon peel, OR preserved ginger OR a few raisins.

(C)
1 Gaily.
2 Eton collars.
3 Shiny.
4 A black satin note.
5 As if their coats were too tight.
6 Audience.
7 Sporadic.
8 "Bloke".

5

(A)
1 Dogs, cats, rats.
2 Salted sprats.
3 Men's Sunday hats.
4 Cheese, soup, salted sprats.
5 Cook.
6 Vats and kegs.
7 Keyboard of a piano or organ.
8 To the Town Hall.
9 A noddy.
10 Dolts.
11 Send them packing.
12 "Quaked with a mighty consternation".

(B)
1 17th March 1958.
2 25th March 1958.
3 25th March 1944.
4 Saturday.
5 Twenty-eight (28) days.
6 Saturday.

(C)
1 Out of a window.
2 Into a high tree.
3 Wings, eye, neck, breast, claws or talons.
4 Beautiful, bright, graceful.
5 To surprise the fox with her voice or "caw".
6 To flattery.
7 Moral.

6

(A)
1 By a blow, knock or fall.
2 Six.
3 A metal spoon, coin or similar object.
4 Salad oil.
5 Cold water and tincture of arnica.
6 Glass.
7 One teaspoonful to a tumbler of water.
8 As soon as possible after receiving the injury.

(B)
1. On the Atlantic Ocean.
2. Sailor.
3. His grandfather.
4. Ancestors.
5. At sea.
6. Disinherit.
7. A roving disposition.
8. In a fishing village on the west coast of England.
9. Because it was on the shores of the sea which for so many years had been his home.

(C)
1. Barraques.
2. Near Dover Castle.
3. Just over half an hour.
4. *The Daily Mail* £1,000 prize.
5. Britain's insular safety.
6. He was flooded with orders from many Governments.
7. The 50-horse-power "Gnome" rotary engine.
8. Hubert Latham.

7

(A)
1. A flawn.
2. Refectory.
3. Rheims in France, Namur in Belgium.
4. Lavender-water and Eau de Cologne.
5. To wipe the hands of the Pope.
6. Lavender-water and Eau de Cologne.
7. The Cardinal's hat marked in "permanent ink".
8. A jug or pitcher.

(B)
1. A grindstone.
2. By striking it with steel.
3. Nose, cheek, eyes, lips, head, eyebrows, chin.
4. Red, blue.
5. Internal.
6. Grating. A kind of grid (or similar answer).
7. The hottest part of the year, usually in July and August, when dogs are prone to bite and be bad-tempered.
8. Freeze.
9. They often "came down" handsomely.
10. A small sum of money. A sponge cake soaked in wine and custard.
11. What time it was.
12. How to find their way to any special place.
13. Rime. Hoar frost.
14. The cold within him.

(C)
1. Wednesday.
2. Friday's child.
3. Thursday's child.
4. Monday's child.
5. Saturday's child.
6. The child's birthday.
7. A superstition.

8

(A)
1. For shifting coal.
2. 1825.
3. The price of coal at Darlington fell nearly ten shillings (per ton).
4. Atomic power.
5. Canal owners and land owners.
6. Cattle would be poisoned by the smoke, crops damaged, and hayricks set on fire by sparks from the engine.
7. Trade would be taken away from the canal owners and the peace of the countryside ruined.
8. George Stephenson.
9. Opponents.
10. Unconvinced.
11. Locomotive.
12. Tremendous.
13. Timid or fearful.
14. Prophesied.

(B)
1. Walsingham.
2. Forty.
3. Red-gold hair, clear complexion, steady eyes under arched brows, thin curved nose, high cheek-bones and long chin.
4. She liked to probe their minds.
5. "Drake saw into men".
6. Of medium or "middle" height.
7. Both had a fine brain and a will of iron.

(C)
1. A spring.
2. Christian and two others.
3. Christian.
4. He told himself to pluck up courage.
5. A narrow road.
6. Danger and Destruction.
7. Danger led to a great wood; Destruction led to a wide field full of dark mountains.

9

(A)
1. Nine hours.
2. On the grass.
3. The threads which bound him.
4. Upwards.
5. A confused noise.
6. Barely six inches.
7. Bow and arrow and quiver.
8. Forty.
9. Roared loudly.
10. They all leapt back from off his body.

(B)
1. In Sherwood Forest.
2. He was on his way back to England after his captivity.
3. A clergyman or man in Holy Orders.
4. Discontent.
5. The Sheriff of Nottingham.
6. Friar Tuck and Little John.
7. The Sheriff of Nottingham and his men.
8. People who rent land or property.
9. They played in archery contests, bouts of arms and at quarter-staff.

(C)
1. Thirty-five years.
2. Twenty-eight years, two months and nineteen days.
3. 19th December, 1686.
4. By the ship's account.
5. 11th June, 1687.
6. From 19th December, 1686, to 11th June, 1687. Just under six months.
7. A goat's skin cap, umbrella, one parrot, money.
8. For relics.

10

(A)
1. Tar oil winter wash.
2. Nicotine.
3. Tar oil winter wash.
4. Derris powder.
5. Nicotine spray.
6. Burgundy mixture and Bordeaux mixture.
7. To pour water on the lime.

(B)
1. Lord Tweedsmuir.
2. Governor-General of Canada.
3. Scottish.
4. A crazy folly.
5. Ruins.
6. Huns and Boche.
7. In a woodcutter's cottage.
8. To be able to laugh and to be merciful.

(B)—*Contd.*

9 Her face had the skin stretched tight over the bones and it was almost transparent.
10 She sacrificed her own food to them.
11 Africa.
12 He told them long yarns about Africa, lions and tigers, and made them wooden toys, a monkey, a springbok, and a rhinoceros.

(C)

1 It implied that he was a coward.
2 Three.
3 Three letters.
4 Its absence of weight.
5 Flakes of snow.
6 Whiter than the white feathers.
7 Some perplexity but loyal confidence.

11

(A)

1 In Venice.
2 By lending money at great interest to Christian merchants.
3 Hard-hearted.
4 Antonio, a young merchant of Venice.
5 Because he lent money free of interest to people in distress. He also upbraided Shylock.
6 The Rialto.
7 The Stock Exchange.
8 With his usuries and hard dealings.
9 (a) covetous (b) enmity (c) meditated (d) amassed.

(B)

1 Molten rock flowing from a volcano which afterwards solidifies.
2 Jupiter.
3 About fifty.
4 Remarkably plain.
5 High and bald.
6 Brown.
7 Small receptacle for ink, a stilus for writing, and tablets.
8 A purse.
9 The forehead. The summit or brow of a hill.
10 Rather gay with colours of scarlet and purple.

(C)

1 Between forty and fifty.
2 With his elder brother as superintendent of his game.

(C)—*Contd.*

3 Hunts a pack of dogs.
4 On account of his ancient family.
5 He is able to make an artificial fly for fishing to perfection.
6 A puppy.
7 All the young heirs of the county.
8 He was probably a younger son and would not inherit any estate.

12

(A)

1 The animal world.
2 Stay one minute in a field by themselves.
3 Try to break the rack and manger and leap out of a stable window.
4 Oxen, cows, sheep.
5 A baby deer.
6 A herd of dairy cows.
7 A chase ensued.
8 (a) Propensity (b) species (c) menacing (d) assailants.
9 (a) Where hay is, stored a box or trough in the stable where the hay is put for the horse to eat.
  (b) Fierce noises made by angry cows.
  (c) A chase followed or took place.

(B)

1 London.
2 Early morning.
3 Tower of London and dome of St. Paul's Cathedral.
4 Because the towers, etc., lay "open unto the fields".
5 Smokeless.
6 (a) "the very houses seem asleep."
  (b) "It glideth at his own sweet will."
7 Flood with sunlight.

(C)

1 Because he had to live in inns and was drained of his money very rapidly.
2 One.
3 Of coffee and tea.
4 He ate blackberries, hips and haws.
5 Wrote business letters for cottagers and love-letters for young women.
6 With hospitality.
7 Wales.
8 Shrewsbury.
9 (a) Constant practice or rule.
  (b) Now and again.
  (c) With generosity or kindness.

13

(A)
1. At the copper.
2. Gruel.
3. A long grace.
4. Short commons.
5. By asking for more.
6. Fat and healthy.
7. (a) Conclave.
   (b) Pinioned.
   (c) Dietary.
8. That Oliver would be hung.
9. Horror.
10. His cook's uniform.

(B)
1. Make-up or cosmetics.
2. A rose-petal.
3. Large and dark with long lashes.
4. Because she pushed it back under her round cap.
5. Shape.
6. A geographical term meaning a line on a map joining all points which are the same height above sea-level.
7. It was made of linen and used when she was making butter.
8. "Conjure up the image of."
9. A distracting kitten-like maiden.

(C)
1. In his lair.
2. By running over his nose.
3. (a) Unconsciously.
   (b) Insignificant.
4. Ranging the woods for his prey.
5. He found himself entangled.
6. Set up a roar.
7. A kind of net with ropes.
8. He nibbled the knot in the cord which bound the lion.
9. One good turn deserves another, or some such phrase as at the end of the fable.

14

(A)
1. He would be severely stung, or similar answer.
2. He should deftly apply a little smoke and be gentle and careful in his movements.
3. Some natural catastrophe to which they will do well to submit.
4. Rush to their reserves of honey.
5. They would want to possess the material for starting a new city immediately.
6. (a) Skilful, dexterous, or handle neatly.
   (b) A disaster.
   (c) To leave or desert.

(B)
1. The wonderful milk or intelligence of the Alderney cow.
2. Because it tumbled into a lime pit.
3. A bath of oil.
4. Because it had a droll appearance.
5. Impossible to tell.
6. True.
7. Not true.
8. In the Channel Islands.

(C)
1. Because they were stiff.
2. Theatrical lumber and old clothes.
3. Tumble-down, damp, and rat-infested.
4. Because he heard a noise.
5. Old-fashioned.
6. (a) Odds and ends of stage property left by actors.
   (b) Rummaging.
   (c) Swarming with rats.
7. It is impossible to tell.
8. Not true.
9. True.
10. Impossible to tell.

15

(A)
1. Provides raw material for pulp and paper industries.
2. Frozen state of ground facilitates transport.
3. Electric power.
4. From rivers and lakes.
5. Michigan, Huron, Erie, Superior, Ontario.
6. Fur trapping.
7. Montreal, Winnipeg, Edmonton, New York, St. Louis, London.

(B)
1. A very high death-rate.
2. Bacteria.
3. Carbolic acid.
4. All instruments, bandages, hands of surgeon and nurses.
5. A fall in death-rate from blood-poisoning.
6. Anti-septic surgery.
7. Dettol, iodine, permanganate of potash, methylated spirits, etc.
8. By heating and boiling.
9. 'Sterilising' and 'disinfecting'.
10. Pasteur.

(C)
1. Kneeling.
2. With silent resignation.
3. Turns round her supple neck, looks sadly upon the increasing load, sighs or weeps.
4. A quilt or carpet folded.

11

(C)—*Contd.*

    5 He used his stirrups to support his dangling legs.
    6 'Suspicion'.
    7 'To resign'.
    8 Impatient.
    9 (a) Adverb.
       (b) Adjective.
  10 'Remonstrates'.

16

(A)

    1 He was on his rambles, or similar answer.
    2 At first rather narrow but later widened out with ruts and trees.
    3 Ancient oaks.
    4 The branches projected and met overhead forming a canopy.
    5 A kind of low tent or booth.
    6 Thin smoke.
    7 A couple of light carts with two or three horses beside.
    8 (a) Sward or herbage.
       (b) Cauldron.
       (c) Cropping.
    9 (a) Retreated (b) Above (c) Shallow (d) Gently.

(B)

    1 Magnificent.
    2 At Aldgate.
    3 They were covered with gravel and railed on either side.
    4 Jane (Lady Jane Grey).
    5 Members of the Craft Guilds.
    6 Officers of the Guard and attendants.
    7 The Tower of London.
    8 Roofs, walls, gables and steeples.
    9 (a) Preparations.
       (b) Staves.
       (c) Richly-attired.
  10 Usurper.

(C)

    1 Singularly beautiful.
    2 Corunna.
    3 Early summer.
    4 Galleons.
    5 With long streamers and red crosses.
    6 Fruit boats and pinnaces.
    7 30,000.
    8 20,000.
    9 (a) Loiterers.
       (b) Interval.
       (c) Remnant.

17

(A)

    1 A bell which rang from very early times to say that all fires and lights should be put out.

(A)—*Contd.*

2 Lea.
3 'The ploughman homeward plods his weary way.'
4 (a) Owl (b) Beetle (c) Cows and sheep.
5 'Now fades the glimmering landscape on the sight.'
6 Moping and solitary.
7 Beneath the elm trees and yew tree's shade.
8 In an ivy-mantled tower.

(B)

1 The seas around South America originally belonging to Spain. 'Main' really meant 'strength'.
2 One sheet of living flame.
3 Ten thousand, an indefinitely great number.
4 19,000 feet.
5 Venus.
6 The heavens, the hills, the sea.
7 Emeralds and rubies.
8 Gold and silver.
9 (a) Cone (b) Depth (c) Soil (d) Dull (e) Tinges.

(C)

1 In the Atlantic Ocean.
2 A sailing ship.
3 A heavy gale.
4 Front.
5 Back.
6 A good seaman.
7 Providence.
8 Before the wheel.
9 Because the helm requires great attention when the ship is running before a gale.
10 "All above us one *black* sky".
11 (a) Whether (b) Canvass (c) Sale (d) Witch.

18

(A)

1 Travelling in a railway carriage.
2 (a) Time worth a thousand pounds a minute.
 (b) Land . . . . . an inch
 (c) Smoke . . . . . . a puff
 (d) Language . . .. a word
3 Because it was mentioned so much.
4 Telescope and opera glasses.
5 Microscope.
6 Her ticket.
7 That she should have bought her ticket from the engine driver.
8 They were about the same size as the people and seemed to fill the carriage.
9 (a) Have not (b) was not (c) do not (d) I am.
10 (a) There's (b) didn't (c) hadn't (d) you're.

(B)
1. With a red cross.
2. The Crusaders.
3. The bells tolling.
4. Carts which carried dead bodies.
5. Dogs and cats.
6. They were ordered to be destroyed.
7. Most were drowned in the Thames and washed ashore and their decaying bodies helped to spread the disease.
8. A kind of washable paint.
9. Obverse.
10. (a) Infection (b) melancholy or lamentable (c) noxious (d) effluvium.

(C)
1. French.
2. Interpreted.
3. Yes.
4. Struck him under the ear.
5. Middle Ages.
6. Forks and flesh-hooks.
7. With a great broach or spit.
8. As a boy against the monks of Peterborough.
9. At Brandon.
10. The Wake or the Last of the English. The Isle of Ely in the Fens.

19

(A)
1. He had little or no money and he had nothing in particular to interest him on shore.
2. It would drive off the spleen and regulate his circulation.
3. A purse with something in it.
4. They get sea-sick, grow quarrelsome, don't sleep at nights and don't enjoy themselves.
5. As a member of the crew.
6. Commodore and Captain.
7. (The teacher will mark these).
8. Funeral and coffin.
9. A sailor.
10. Damp and drizzly.
11. With his soul.

(B)
1. A swine-herd.
2. Collected mast for his hogs.
3. A great lubberly boy.
4. Playing with fire.
5. (a) Old-fashioned or ancient. (b) Lighting or setting fire to. (c) A building.
6. A litter of nine new-farrowed pigs.
7. The loss of the pigs.
8. (a) Proper noun (b) Verb (c) Adverb (d) Adjective.

(C)
1. At the harbour mouth at low tide.
2. Fifty to sixty.
3. Round and white, slightly smaller than an English walnut.
4. It tripped them up and greatly increased their fun.
5. Their faces turned away.
6. They came up blowing, sputtering, laughing, and gasping for breath.
7. (a) A kind of sweet eaten at parties or as a second course at dinner.
   (b) Trees found in tropical countries.
   (c) Flower arrangements.
8. After dinner; on Friday morning; after breakfast; that night.

20

(A)
1. Because the Norman archers were shooting their arrows into the sky.
2. He was killed by an arrow which pierced his eye.
3. To fight on and conceal his death.
4. Simultaneous.
5. A Saxon thane or knight.
6. The falling arrow.
7. The rich silk banner.
8. Corpse.

(B)
1. External and exterior.
2. Twenty feet.
3. River Cher (a tributary).
4. Fosse.
5. An iron palisade or fence.
6. To try and climb over the sharp iron spikes on each pale.
7. Suicide.
8. The donjon-keep.
9. A black Ethiopian giant.
10. Very small, merely shot-holes.

(C)
1. Three chambers.
2. A garden arranged in steps or tiers.
3. In a niche.
4. The fruit.
5. The fruit of each tree had a separate colour.
6. Sparkling and transparent.
7. (a) Emeralds (b) rubies (c) turquoises, (d) amethysts.
8. Pieces of coloured glass.
9. Because they were so brilliant, beautifully coloured and of great size.
10. In his pockets, in his girdle, and inside his shirt.

15

21

(A)
1. Cheetham.
2. In the crow's nest.
3. Latitude 62°.
4. Great masses of sugar.
5. The albatross.
6. The brown-backed petrels.
7. Twenty-seven.
8. Clustered in groups on the forecastle, sketching and painting.
9. Sturdy prow or bows of ship.
10. Huge tabular variety and little weathered water-worn bergs.

(B)
1. Pressmen and others.
2. Taking of photographs.
3. 60 lbs.
4. The metal ladder and aluminium trunk.
5. An ambassador's residence.
6. Because they were on the final stage of their journey; planning had given place to action.
7. Aluminium.
8. Lightness in weight.
9. (a) Formidable (b) dimensions (c) transported.
10. (a) In the Himalayas. (b) 29,141 feet.

(C)
1. The narrow strip of water between the French and English coasts.
2. Hesitated, delayed giving a decision, or similar answer.
3. Stormy.
4. In the hold.
5. They slithered about the wet planking, and got soaked and nervous.
6. Slid about, or slipped.
7. Slowly left the station.
8. A grocer's or general store.
9. Boulogne.
10. Bread.
11. 1914 to 1918.

22

(A)
1. The amount of water in it and its low heating value.
2. In bogs and swamps.
3. Because it cannot easily be transported.
4. It will burn slowly and will help to keep the fire in if it is put on top of a large piece of coal.
5. Nine-tenths water.
6. Adjective, moist; verb, moisten. Adjective, original; verb, originate.

(B)
1. (a) A reddish soil which contains exactly the elements which coffee requires.
   (b) High altitudes.
   (c) Plenty of sunshine to dry the coffee.
   (d) Nearness to the coast makes transport easy and inexpensive.

2. (a) Descend (b) inconvenient (c) inferior (d) moistening, wetting, or damping (e) import.
3. (a) TRUE.
   (b) TRUE.
   (c) UNTRUE.
4. Brazil.
5. South America.

(C)
1. The patent automatic filter switch unit.
2. With the head-lamp switch in the 'on' position.
3. Motionless—not moving.
4. Station*ery*, meaning 'writing materials and paper' bought in a stationer's shop.
5. By three standard dry battery leak-proof cells.
6. From the 'Dynohub'.
7. Because it has no moving parts and requires no service.
8. Impossible to get out of order, or similar answer.
9. Keeps usage of battery current to a minimum and ensures long battery life.
10. (a) Running stream or in general circulation.
    (b) Curr*ant*. A kind of fruit often found in buns and cakes.
    (c) Maximum.

23

(A)
1. King's baker's house, Pudding Lane.
2. Down to the water-side.
3. By flinging them into the river or into boats.
4. Their wings were burnt and they fell down.
5. A high wind.
6. A drought.
7. Some of the houses should be pulled down.
8. In 'White Hall'.
9. Elborough, a parson.
10. The Great Plague.

(B)
1. France.
2. From Deptford to Dartford.
3. Common land fenced round.
4. Some 'shabby-genteel' houses.

(B)—*Contd.*

5 That they were rather ridiculous.
6 Barracks, magazines, martello-towers.
7 Cattle, sheep, pigs, and geese.
8 Heath, furze, and turf.
9 (a) Adjective (b) noun (c) verb (d) adverb (e) pronoun.

(C)

1 A stone cross marking the site where the market was held and from where speakers addressed the crowd.
2 Lancashire.
3 Utterly wild.
4 To push him down.
5 A sermon or address.
6 A stone struck him on the cheek.
7 A stone hit him on the forehead.
8 Upon the joints of his fingers.
9 To God.
10 Wesleyans or Methodists.

24

(A)

1 "Familiarity breeds contempt."
2 Because he knows it will probably rain.
3 It is either too dry or too wet.
4 Because it so often brings thunder-storms which spoil his crops.
5 Because a wet autumn is happily uncommon.
6 Ploughing, hedging and ditching, and tidying-up.
7 Because there is a brief lull in his eternal battle against Time.
8 Lays flat the unripe corn, spoils the hay and delays the harvest.

(B)

1 They are equipped with stings.
2 Formic acid.
3 They first bite it and then spray poison into the wound.
4 They eject their formic acid into the air from points of vantage.
5 Pungent fumes tend to drive away the foe.
6 (a) Venom (b) aperture (c) cumbersome (d) disconcert (e) eject or squirt.
7 A cloud of pungent fumes.
8 A reservoir.

(C)
1. Germany and France.
2. By the law which forbade any vehicle to exceed 4 miles an hour and that each one had to be preceded by a man carrying a red flag.
3. As a mere joke or as dangerous playthings.
4. Noisy, clumsy, queer-looking things.
5. In 1888 when Carl Benz produced the three-wheeled internal-combustion car.
6. Daimler.
7. About 8 to 10 miles per hour.
8. Rolls-Royce, Austin, Morris, Ford, etc.
9. Light in weight; small in size; fuel burnt in it as waste.
10. Revoked or abolished.

25

(A)
1. The Custom House.
2. To see if they had any contraband articles.
3. The date of the coronation had been suddenly advanced.
4. All the rooms were let and hotels overflowing.
5. A very heavy price.
6. At Zenda.
7. Monday.
8. Wander over the hills and look at the Castle.
9. Features or facial expression of the Elphbergs, the Royal Family.

(B)
1. Because they were exhausted by an endless life of fatigue and peril.
2. A number of noisy, vapouring people.
3. Empty bubbles.
4. -------- ----make most noise."
5. They were too great to be endured.
6. More than fifty.
7. Beasts of burden.
8. With perfect composure.
9. Caesar, Napoleon, Wellington, Marlborough, Wolfe, etc.
10. "Vain" meaning "proud", OR "Vane" as in "weather-vane".

(C)
1. About fifty-five.
2. Because his hair was silver white.
3. The harshness of his features and voice.
4. Inelegant, unclassic, unaristocratic.
5. Vulgar.
6. For its pith, sagacity, intelligence and originality.

(C)—*Contd.*

7 He is described as a man 'difficult to lead and impossible to drive'.
8 Well-made and wiry.
9 'There was not a suspicion of the clown about him anywhere.'
10 (a) 'Mould' may mean 'loose earth' or a 'vessel in which jellies, puddings or metal are cast to give them shape'.
  (b) 'Furrow' is the line left by a plough.
11 (a) Shrewd, intelligent.
  (b) Honesty, uprightness.
  (c) Distinctive features.

26

(A)
1 They were praying.
2 Ten miles.
3 Brussels in Belgium.
4 The Duke of Wellington.
5 Napoleon.
6 The Imperial Guard.
7 Unscared by the thunder of the English artillery.
8 On a hill.
9 "The French column pressed on and *up the hill* and seemed almost *to crest the eminence.*"
10 "Receiving and repelling the furious charges of the French cavalry."
11 (a) Dauntless (b) furious.

(B)
1 Winter.
2 3 o'clock in the afternoon.
3 Wild roses in summer, nuts and blackberries in autumn.
4 Red and brown.
5 The path was paved with stones.
6 Because it was winter and the cattle would be inside.
7 Little brown birds.
8 Its utter solitude.
9 (a) Hard (b) still (c) lonely.
10 Setting.

(C)
1 "To weigh and consider."
2 To be read only in parts.
3 With diligence and attention.
4 They can be "read by deputy and extracts made of them by others."
5 It makes him an exact man.
6 A good memory.
7 He must pretend to know a lot.
8 He should be able to argue or contend.

(C)—*Contd.*

9 (a) Acting for some one else.
 (b) Water which is clarified or freed from impurities.
 (c) A meeting where conversation is important.
 (d) The science of reasoning.

These or similar answers should be accepted.

27

(A)
1 Buckinghamshire.
2 (a) With good prospects, or similar answer.
 (b) Friendly and polite manner.
3 Sports, exercises, and company.
4 Cheerfulness, vivacity, courtesy.
5 "The business of ship-money".
6 "With rare temper and modesty".
7 Knight of the Shire for his county.
8 As their 'Country's Father'.
9 Threatened by tempests and rocks.

(B)
1 A building.
2 Encrusted with marble and decorated with statues.
3 From sixty to eighty.
4 80,000.
5 Sixty-four.
6 Because they would 'vomit forth' the people.
7 By a canopy.
8 By the continual playing of fountains and the spraying of aromatics.
9 An arena or stage strewed with sand.
10 A wide lake.

(C)
1 Bradshaw's Court.
2 Refused to plead.
3 Thirty-two.
4 To satisfy the consciences of the judges.
5 The fifth day.
6 With dignity and courage.
7 Before the Banqueting House, Whitehall.
8 30th January, 1649.
9 Oliver Cromwell.

28

(A)
1 Animal, casein, and resin.
2 It is free from any tendency to stain.
 It is neither heat nor water proof.
3 It must be used hot.

(A)—*Contd.*

4 Put in a piece of sacking and broken up small with a hammer.
5 Overnight.
6 It should run freely from the brush.
7 To prevent the glue from chilling.
8 In a warm shop.
9 Cramps, cramp shoe-blocks, and testing tools.
10 It should be wiped off at once before it sets hard.

(B)
1 1822.
2 A tanner, who was a soldier in Napoleon's army.
3 To the study of germs, microbes or bacteria.
4 Little rod-shaped organisms.
5 In the air, water, and soils, and in the bodies of animals and plants.
6 Convert matter into food for plants.
7 Brewing, the silk industry, agriculture.
8 A worker in leather.

(C)
1 For freeing the slaves of America.
2 The Saviour of American Union.
3 Darwin, Tennyson, and Gladstone.
4 Darwin, a scientist famous for evolution.
Tennyson, a poet.
Gladstone, a statesman.
5 The Quakers.
6 War and violence.
7 The horrors of Civil War.
8 To save the American Union.
9 A settlement agreeable to both sides.
10 Washington, Roosevelt, Truman, Eisenhower, etc.
11 The official residence of the President of the U.S.A.

29

(A)
1 27th June, 1787.
2 In a summerhouse, in his garden.
3 He took several turns in a "berceau" or covered walk of acacias.
4 Emotions of joy.
5 Fame.
6 He felt sorry that he "had taken an everlasting leave of an old and agreeable companion'.
7 It must be "short and precarious".

(A)—*Contd.*

8 Flowering trees.
9 "The air was temperate, the sky was serene, the silver orb of the moon was reflected from the waters and all nature was silent."
10 (a) To disguise or conceal.
    (b) Perilous, uncertain.

(B)

1 Holywood.
2 The followers of Lord Foxham, and the followers of Dick who were outlaws.
3 Lord Foxham. He was conveyed to the Abbey.
4 Money.
5 Rated them for poltroonery.
6 The Goat and Bagpipes.
7 (a) Disappear.
  (b) Volunteers.
  (c) Prolonged.
  (d) Courage.
  (e) Separated.
8 (a) Stupidity or cowardice.
  (b) Sullen.
  (c) Disappear.
  (d) Severally.

(C)

1 A magazine or newspaper.
2 Dr. Johnson's Dictionary.
3 The Earl of Chesterfield.
4 So that he should recommend the Dictionary.
5 He was repulsed.
6 After it was published.
7 One who gives support or shows favour, or similar answer.
8 Sarcastic.
9 Seven years.

30

(A)

1 Wild with expectation.
2 By a dove.
3 Mayor.
4 The Spaniards.
5 Lammen.
6 A sally, sudden attack or similar phrase.
7 Toward, yonder, behind, before, against.
8 Pitch-black.
9 A long procession of lights issuing from the fort.
10 That between the Cow-gate and the Tower of Burgundy.
11 The Spaniards attacking them.
12 A desperate sortie of the citizens.

(B)

1 "Some lineaments of the character of the man were early discerned in the child."

(B)—*Contd.*

2 Fighting.
3 Market-Drayton.
4 Shropshire.
5 Climbed the church steeple.
6 (a) Reprobate.
 (b) Compatible.
 (c) Sagacious.
 (d) Predatory.

7 To save their windows from being broken.
8 That he would make a great figure in the world.
9 That he was a dunce if not a reprobate.
10 Prophecy.

(C)
1 In the parish of Oare in the county of Somerset.
2 Churchwarden.
3 To clear the name of the parish from ill fame and calumny.
4 A plain unlettered man.
5 Yeomen.
6 Well-read in foreign languages.

7 William Shakespeare.
8 'I trow' or 'to wit'.
9 A very ignorant person, or as John Ridd says, "A plain unlettered man".
10 A flat piece of land as used in geography.

31

(A)
1 They broke a cup.
2 On top of a tomato.
3 The butter.
4 The pies.
5 One and twopence (a pound).

6 Salt.
7 In the kettle.
8 The tomato.
9 Because they couldn't find a trace of the butter.
10 In the teapot.

(B)
1 Between thirteen and fourteen.
2 Eight years old.
3 Orphans.
4 They had been under little or no restraint, and only attended to by servants.
5 Benjamin the man of the house, and old Jacob Armitage.
6 Very exacting and had 'a high notion of her own consequence'.
7 Three in all.
8 Ten.
9 (a) Boisterous.
 (b) Independent.

(C)
1. Cut in two a bar of iron.
2. To cut in halves a young tree.
3. No.
4. De Vaux.
5. A famous sword owned by the British King Arthur.
6. Cut in two a silken cushion.
7. As a curved and narrow blade of a dull blue colour.
8. (a) Broad and muscular.
   (b) Thin and spare.
9. A Crusade (The third).
10. The Saracens.

32

(A)
1. As soon as possible after their seven o'clock breakfast.
2. (a) Because they liked plenty of time to play on the road.
   (b) Because their mothers wanted them out of the way before housecleaning began.
3. Flat rush dinner-baskets.
4. Two hot potatoes.
5. Marbles and dibs with pebbles.
6. Slide on the ice on the puddles and make snowballs.
7. They would be 'raided', that is, some of the food would be eaten.
8. The young green leaves from the hawthorn hedges.
9. Sorrel leaves.
10. Haws, blackberries, sloes and crab-apples.
11. 'From habit and relish of the wild food'.

(B)
1. A life story told by the person or object concerned.
2. In a soft, silver sound.
3. Peru.
4. A silver bar.
5. It was conveyed to England in one of Drake's ships as part of his plunder.
6. It was changed into a British coin.
7. It began to ramble in all parts of the country.
8. Miser, the miser's heir.

(C)
1. The world is a stage and the men and women players.
2. A door leading out.
3. Whining, with a satchel, shining morning face, creeping like snail unwillingly to school.
4. The bubble reputation.
5. Stomach well filled with chicken.

(C)—*Contd.*

6 The justice.
7 Wise sayings and modern examples, or similar answer.
8 (a) Lean and slippered pantaloon.
  (b) Spectacles on nose.
  (c) Wide hose too large for his 'shrunk shank'.
  (d) Childish voice, piping and whistling.
  (e) Second childhood, without teeth or taste, and poor eyesight.
9 Without.
10 Treble.

33

(A)
1 Rev. C. L. Dodgson.
2 Lewis Carroll.
3 A pen name, nom de plume, or pseudonym.
4 A lecturer in mathematics at Oxford University.
5 French and music.
6 Because they didn't learn washing.
7 Reading and writing.
8 Addition.
9 Subtraction.
10 Multiplication.
11 Division.
12 Simpleton.

(B)
1 Because Christmas was coming.
2 In Bishopsgate.
3 Whitehall Palace.
4 The Merry Wives of Windsor.
5 With holly, ivy, bays, rosemary, mistletoe, and candles.
6 Falstaff, Anne Page, and Mistress Quickly.
7 Ten pounds, £10.
8 6th January.
9 A ruff.
10 A cascade.

(C)
1 Lest he should slip on the ferns and mosses which covered the stairs.
2 With his back.
3 Because John had an injured leg.
4 Endless galleries cut in the solid rock.
5 Twice.
6 With his tinder box.
7 Through an opening at the far end of the cave.
8 There was a colder air and a fresh salt smell.

34

(A)
1. A small cave.
2. Ice.
3. To make more head room.
4. Took off their boots.
5. Terray, because he had a sleeping bag.
6. Four.
7. Sat on the cine-camera.
8. Sleep close together for warmth.
9. Hypothesis.
10. Protection.

(B)
1. High, steeple-crowned.
2. In the gallery of a theatre.
3. Congregation.
4. Some in corselets and steel caps, some in buff and others in red coats.
5. Pikes and muskets.
6. With courage and resolution.
7. With no small degree of awe.
8. (a) FALSE.
   (b) TRUE.
   (c) TRUE.
   (d) FALSE.
9. Bear-baiting.
10. Resolve.

(C)
1. They were busy, bustling, and disputatious instead of their accustomed quietness.
2. Long grizzled beard, rusty fowling-piece, uncouth dress.
3. An army of women and children.
4. The tavern politicians.
5. An election.
6. Raise a riot in the village.
7. A tory, spy, or refugee.
8. Some neighbours who used to 'keep about the tavern'.
9. (a) Long or grizzled.
   (b) Tranquillity.
   (c) Rip Van Winkle, God.
   (d) Tory.

35

(A)
1. 6 feet by 4 feet.
2. To prevent the exit of small boys and the entrance of contraband articles.
3. Uncommonly comfortable.
4. Three.
5. Tom Crib.
6. A square table, a hard-seated sofa, a good stout wooden chair, bookcases.
7. Grimaldi.
8. Bookcases with cupboards at the bottom.
9. Climbing-irons.
10. A cricket bat and a small fishing rod.

(B)
1 Superlatively fine.
2 Quite cheerful.
3 When he was lower down the mountain.
4 Two-and-a-half-hours.
5 A double eiderdown sleeping bag and a small li-lo.
6 Three tins of sardines, a tongue, and a tin of herrings.
7 Felt-lined climbing boots and four pairs of ordinary socks.
8 A tube of Anti-Lux, sticking plaster, and aspirins.
9 For one week.
10 Twenty pounds.

(C)
1 Gabriel.
2 A young man.
3 His eyes were small, and his mouth was large.
4 On Sundays.
5 He thought of what there would be for dinner.
6 Rather a bad man.
7 For security in high winds.
8 Large and roomy.
9 Ordinary leather leggings.
10 Tantrums.

36

(A)
1 Fairly flat with jungle on either side.
2 They unbolted a section of the metals.
3 In 1895.
4 Murder and pillage by armed robbers.
5 To leave the carriage.
6 He dropped his pistol and ammunition on the floor under the carriage seat.
7 About a dozen.
8 Five.
9 German and Dutch.
10 To produce their money and valuables and place them on the ground.

(B)
1 Masonry.
2 There was plenty of cover.
3 Rails and two uncut wire fences.
4 Forty yards.
5 He lost it while getting on and off the engine.
6 A Mauser.
7 Because he was a newspaper correspondent.
8 Because he was covered by the Boer's rifle and there was no chance of escape.
9 An autobiography.

(C)
1 To applaud the turns.
2 The most popular attraction in the world.
3 Jugglers, girls on horseback, trapeze artistes, tumblers.
4 A loud noise from the band; the ring-master announcing Lazerenko.
5 The most famous clown in all the Russias.
6 On top of the bandstand.
7 An endless stream of old pots and pans which followed Lazerenko as he dived into the ring.
8 How he managed to fall so far without hurting himself.
9 Bertram Mills Circus at Olympia, London, and Bellevue, Manchester.

37

(A)
1 The cattle-market.
2 A horse and trap.
3 Wiltshire.
4 Lisle-thread stockings.
5 Ox Row, Blue Boar Row, Oatmeal Row.
6 Very tall, slender, and graceful, or similar answer.
7 St. Paul's in London and Truro in Cornwall.
8 Covered-in passages often seen in a cathedral or monastery.
9 Dignified.
10 A whisper of organ music.

(B)
1 Social abuses. Victorian period.
2 His heart sank and he gave up hope.
3 That somebody was trying to shoot him.
4 A skein of silk.
5 Lower the silk with his knife attached to it, count one hundred and then draw it up.
6 A stout whip-cord.
7 With his tinder-box.
8 Continually drawing up the heavy rope.
9 He passed it through both handles of the chest.
10 (a) Missiles.
   (b) Despondency.

(C)
1 His shaving.
2 He wore a monocle or eye-glass.
3 He took out his false teeth.
4 Savages.

(C)—*Contd.*

5 He referred to Good's gums as "utterly innocent of ivories as a new-born elephant".
6 Spirits or Gods.

7 Threw himself down on the grass and gave vent to a prolonged howl of terror.
8 (a) Ineffable.
   (b) Transparent.

38

(A)
1 It rushed swiftly at the snake and pulled down its front spines over its face.
2 The snake struck at her nose with an angry hiss.
3 The tail.

4 Half of it.
5 Frogs.
6 A 'V' plainly marked behind the head.
7 To prevent it biting him by reflex action.

(B)
1 His boots.
2 'Going' and 'fool'.
3 Eight weeks.
4 By the farm-yard wall.
5 Maelstrom.
6 They were drowned.
7 To the General.

8 Satisfaction at being proved right. He died happy.
9 He probably had a stroke and died as a result.
10 The desire to be proved right in one's prophecies.

(C)
1 The accumulation of material round the vent.
2 A kind of bowl or hollow at the top.
3 Lava.
4 Tuff.
5 Enormous pressure which sometimes blows part of the mountain away.
6 Vesuvius.
7 Herculaneum and Pompeii, buried 79 A.D.
8 In Italy.

39

(A)
1 In the South Park.
2 Barriers where the people enter and pay money in return for their tickets, or similar answer.
3 The Borough Architect.

(A)—*Contd.*

4 Exhibits of embroidery, table-decorations, cookery, bottled fruits, jam, marmalade and lemon-curd.
5 A fun-fair.
6 A display by horses, jumping and competitions.
7 Because more people are able to attend after work.
8 By the provision of hay and water.
9 The refreshment tent.
10 Exhibits of art, craft, and wild flowers.
11 Tractor, combine harvester and so on.
12 Radio and television sets, electric irons, washing machines.
13 Dogs, rabbits and birds.
14 The sheep-dog trials and exhibition of machinery.
15 Banks on wheels as caravans.
16 The firework display.

(B)
1 Earthly.
2 In the moon jungle.
3 Because they heard the bellowing and grunting noises of the moon-calves drawing near.
4 A spongy mushroom-like growth. They ripped like thin bladders, and emitted a watery humour.
5 Their sphere.
6 (a) Vast, flat calf-like sound.
(b) An amazed and wrathy bellowing.
(c) A clogged bestial sound.
7 Because it was incomplete and inadequate.
8 A crackling and smashing of the scrub.
9 It bent the tops of the bayonet scrub.
10 Shining sides and the long line of its back.

40

(A)
1 A magazine.
2 Watch with mother.
3 Maria Bird.
4 A puppet, because strings are mentioned.
5 Gladys Whitred.
6 Dr. Winifred de Kok, Rose Hacker, Rev. Walter Lane, James Hemming.
7 Problems sent in by viewers.
8 People. The factors which go to make up handwriting, or similar answer.
9 Joan Cambridge.
10 A play in various parts or instalments.
11 Phyllis Bentley.
12 Dick Bamforth and Joe Bamforth.
13 The Cast.

(A)—*Contd.*

14 A kind of chairman or speaker elected by the other members.
15 Out of Doors (Eyes and Ears).
16 Children from Bristol Schools.
17 The West of England Studio.

(B)

1 Underneath and above the body.
2 Hot water in bags or bottles, hot bricks, bags of hot sand, or heated articles.
3 The heat should be carefully checked with the hand to make sure that it is not excessive.
4 At least one layer of cloth or several layers of paper.
5 In the armpits, between the thighs, and along the sides of the trunk.
6 Severe bleeding and unconsciousness.
7 He should be placed comfortably on his back with the head turned fully to one side.
8 Artificial respiration.
9 (a) Too much of anything.
  (b) Breathing produced by mechanical means.
  (c) Clothing which hinders or obstructs breathing.